STRATEGY OF PRAYER

Finding God's Blessings

John A. Harrison

Printed and bound in Canada by Art Bookbindery

www.ArtBookbindery.com

ISBN 978-0-9809781-1-7

Books by John Harrison

Lifestyle of Prayer: Gaining God's Favour (2008)
Strategy of Prayer: Finding God's Blessings (2010)

Next book in the series:

Patterns of Prayer: Enjoying God's Presence

To contact the author for seminars, speaking engagements, and other information please email him at pastorjohn@mts.net.

To order books or find store locations please visit:

www.pastorjohn.ca

“Can we use another book on prayer? You bet we can. Until prayer becomes the rhythm and soul of a believer's life we can use all the encouragement we can get to pray. John Harrison has written a very encouraging book to invite us to pray. It's inspirational, it's informative, it's motivating. Let me invite you to read *Strategy of Prayer*. Better yet use the book as a helpful study guide for your small group or prayer group.”

Jamey McDonald
Executive Director
Baptist General Conference of Canada

“As a man of prayer I have found John Harrison’s latest book *Strategy of Prayer: Finding God's Blessings*, encouraging and challenging. It has been a blessing in my life, and in my conversations with the Lord.”

Mark Hidlebaugh
Chaplain Coordinator
Billy Graham Evangelistic Association

“A good read and very understandable.”

Pam Vesa
Congregational Member
New Life Church, Stonewall, MB

TABLE OF CONTENTS

ACKNOWLEDGMENTS

Writing a book takes a lot of time, effort, resources, and revisions. There is always one more sentence you can rework, story to add, or paragraph to rearrange. But at some point you must stop and publish the work.

In this second book on the series of prayer I would like to express heartfelt thanks to the following people who have helped make this book happen:

First I want to thank my parents, Bill and Elnor Harrison, who continue to daily pray for my ministry and support me in my endeavours. I am given courage to pursue God's dreams in my life, because I know they are praying for me.

I am grateful for my spiritual family at New Life Church, for the inspiration, encouragement and support that I receive, and for the stories of prayer that I am able to include in this book. They are an awesome congregation to serve!

I appreciate Jamey McDonald, Executive Director of the Baptist General Conference for taking time out of his busy schedule to read the manuscript and offer encouraging words. He is a great leader to serve under.

I am thankful to Mark Hidlebaugh, my newest Director of Prayer at New Life Church, for his words of encouragement on this manuscript. It will be a pleasure to work alongside him.

To the staff at Art Bookbindery for the excellent finished product they put together. I appreciate their professionalism.

Again thanks to Pam Vesa for taking time to proofread another book of mine and provide me with invaluable suggestions, corrections, and feedback. She always catches things that I miss.

To my children, Jennica, Melaina, and Carter, who motivate me to put into words for the next generation the thoughts that God lays on my heart and mind. It is to them that I love to teach and guide in learning the lifestyle and strategy of prayer.

Finally and most importantly I am thank my wife, Marcy, for giving me time to write this book. I am deeply grateful for her support of my endeavours.

INTRODUCTION

Some months ago I was asked to read a poem called "The Difference" at a Men's Breakfast. It captures the essence of what I wish to reflect on about the strategy of prayer in this book.

I got up early one morning
and rushed right into the day;
I had so much to accomplish
I didn't have time to pray.

Problems just tumbled about me,
and heavier came each task.
"Why doesn't God help me?" I wondered.
He answered, "You didn't ask."

I wanted to see joy and beauty,
but the day toiled on, gray and bleak;
I wondered why God didn't show me.
He said, "But you didn't seek."

I tried to come into God's presence;
I used all my keys at the lock.
God gently and lovingly chided,
"My child, you didn't knock."

I woke up early this morning, and
paused before entering the day;
I had so much to accomplish
that I had to take time to pray.

-Author Unknown

Effective prayer is not simply a passive recital of words, but an active response in working alongside God to meet the daily needs and conditions we see around us. In the gospel of Luke we read that the disciples asked Jesus to teach them how to pray. Jesus responds by teaching them a pattern for prayer and then shares a short parable to teach them the process of prayer. He wants them to understand that prayer is not passive, but active. It is a process. In Luke 11:5-10 we read

> 5Then he said to them, "Suppose one of you has
> a friend, and he goes to him at midnight and
> says, 'Friend, lend me three loaves of bread,
> 6because a friend of mine on a journey has come
> to me, and I have nothing to set before him.'
>
> 7Then the one inside answers, 'Don't bother me.
> The door is already locked, and my children are
> with me in bed. I can't get anything.' 8I tell you,
> though he will not get up and give him the bread
> because he is his friend, yet because of the man's
> boldness he will get up and give him as much as
> he needs.
>
> 9So I say to you: Ask and it will be given to you;
> seek and you will find; knock and the door will
> be opened to you. 10For everyone who asks
> receives; he who seeks finds; and to him who
> knocks, the door will be opened. (NIV)

In the chapters to follow I wish to focus on this parable and especially verse nine that outlines the process of prayer—ask, seek, knock.

The Greek structure of this verse reveals a continuous action that is involved in prayer. In Greek it reads: "Keep on asking, and you will keep on receiving; keep on seeking, and you will keep on finding; keep on knocking and the door will keep on opening to you."

Prayer is an ongoing process to determine the will of God and his best for your life. I pray that your journey with God will be a rewarding and exciting adventure as you learn to ask of him, seek his answers, and knock to determine his direction.

PRESENT YOUR DESIRES THROUGH ASKING

Overcoming Barriers in Asking

"You do not have, because you do not ask God."
-James 4:2c, NIV

You will never know until you ask. That applies to anything in life. I would never know how to use a computer if I did not ask others or read books to show me how. I would not be married today if I never risked asking my wife on a few dates. I would not be able to play saxophone as well as I do today if I never asked questions from my teacher.

You may have needs and desires in your life, but these will not be met until you learn the art of asking. You will never know the things God wants to give you if you never ask.

In the parable on prayer in Luke 11, Jesus said, "Suppose one of you has a friend, and he goes to him at midnight and says, 'Friend, lend me three loaves of bread, because a friend of mine on a journey has come to me, and I have nothing to set before him'" (vs. 5-6). It makes me curious to know how long it took for this man to ask his neighbour for bread. Why did he come at midnight? Did the friend on his journey arrive so late that midnight was the man's only option, or was he, like us, afraid to ask his neighbour earlier? Did his pride get in the way where he may have thought, "I don't want to appear poor and needy?" Did he feel guilty about burdening his neighbour with a problem of his own? Or was he afraid that his friend would reject his request for help?

Whatever the reason for coming at midnight the man finally lays aside any fear, guilt, or pride he has and humbles himself. He makes the decision to ask because he knows his neighbour is his friend.

What makes it hard for you to request things of God? What keeps you from approaching God? What makes you afraid to talk to God and to share your needs with him? If you are to learn the art of asking, then you must overcome four critical barriers in asking for God's blessings on your life.

Overcome the Risk of Rejection

"Whoever comes to me I will never drive away."
-John 6:37b, NIV

Some people do not ask God, because they fear they will be rejected in their request. Is this a fear that you have? Do you feel you will be turned down, because the request is too dumb, too big, or too insignificant for God?

One of the first hurdles you need to overcome is an unhealthy belief that God is out to harm you. Jeremiah 29:11 says, "'For I know the plans I have for you,'" declares the Lord, "'plans to prosper you and not to harm you, plans to give you hope and a future.'" God is compassionate. His intent is not to keep you in a state of misery, but to release you into a life of goodness. God is not in the business of rejecting anyone who comes to him in sincerity and purity of motive. Jesus said that "whoever comes to me I will never drive away."[1]

God loves to answer your prayers and bring joy into your life, especially those prayers that move you or someone else closer to his will. Yet this does not mean that God always answers your request as you want. If the thing you ask for is a temporary pleasure that will bring future disaster God will reject the request, but still accept you.

I know, as a parent, I would never want to give into a request from my child that would bring disaster upon them. I would be less than a loving father if I gave into every whim and wish of my children knowing it was not in their best interest. God is the same. Sometimes it is in your requests not being answered as you want that reveal God's love and protection on your life. To illustrate this point…

> A lone shipwreck survivor on an uninhabited island managed to build a rude hut in which he placed all that he had saved from his sinking ship. He prayed to God for deliverance, and anxiously watched the horizon each day to hail any passing ship.
>
> One day he was horrified to find his hut in flames. All that he had was gone. To the man's limited vision, it was the worst that could happen, and he cursed God. Yet the very next day a ship arrived.
>
> "We saw your smoke signal!" the captain told him.[2]

God hears your prayers. At times, however, he responds to them in ways that seem to go against the way you think they should be answered. Like this shipwrecked man, God's answer might come in a way that is outside the specifics of what you wanted, but in the end still met the thing you needed most. Be open and alert to how God might be working. Trust him. He hears you and wants to grant your request.

At other times it might be in timing. We want it now, but God knows we do not have the maturity, skills, or ability to handle what we ask for. And so our request is denied. From our perspective what seem like denials to our prayers are to God simply delays.

> At five years old I think my son Carter would be able to turn on the ignition of our van and even possibly put it into gear. If he asked me if he could drive the van it would be ludicrous for me to give Carter the keys and say go ahead. I want him to drive, but not yet! First he needs to grow so he can see over the dashboard and reach the gas pedal and brakes. He also needs to learn the rules of the road, have knowledge of the van, and develop confidence and ability in driving. My desire is that he will drive one day, but in a way that will not be disastrous to him or others.

What is it you have asked but have not yet received? What does God want you to learn or develop in your life? Is it relationship principles and attitudes before you find a marriage partner? Is it some skill, course, or ability before you take on that job you always desire?

Don't give up on prayer just because what you ask for is not granted immediately. God still remembers and wants to give you your heart's desire, but first he wants to bring you to a point of maturity so that what he gives will not be abused and used for self-glory.

Overcome the Sense of Guilt

> *"I said, 'I will confess my transgressions to the LORD'—and you forgave the guilt of my sin. Therefore let everyone who is godly pray to you."*
>
> *-Psalm 32:5b-6a, NIV*

Appropriate guilt is a mechanism of your heart that God uses to restore your relationship with him and others through repentance and forgiveness. Without feelings of guilt you would continue to hurt the other individual and God. It is guilt that reminds you of what has been done wrong and what is needed to make it right.

Yet guilt forgiven should never become a barrier in asking God for the things he places on your heart. Some people struggle with asking God for something special that they messed up earlier in their life. It might be the desire for a marriage partner, but because of past guilt over a failed marriage, some people hesitate, thinking God would never grant them this request. Other people shy away from God because of feelings of unworthiness. Yet it is in the death of Christ on the cross that reveals the depth of a person's worth to God.

Some people I talk to feel guilty over praying to God for their own wants, because they feel it is too selfish. You may miss God's best in your life, because you feel you must live an ascetic lifestyle that denies every good thing that God wants to offer you from this material world. God has created the good things that this world has to offer, and as such you should feel free to receive them from God. 1 Timothy 4:4-5 states "for everything God created is good, and nothing is to be rejected if it is received with thanksgiving, because it is consecrated by the word of God and prayer."

In teaching his disciples how to pray Jesus removes any false guilt over praying for needs, wants, and desires. In this pattern of prayer Jesus tells them to ask God to "give us today our daily bread."[3] You do not have to feel guilty that your request will burden God or is selfish in nature. God will let you know if what you ask for is too selfish or greed-oriented. As James 4:3 says, "When you ask, you do not receive, because you ask with wrong motives, that you may spend what you get on your pleasures." But until you ask you will never know. So go ahead and ask God!

- Ask God for that job promotion you desire.

- Ask God for that companion you long to be with.

- Ask God for a good return on your investments.

- Ask God for that baby you want to have.

Overcome the Attitude of Pride

> *"If my people, who are called by my name, will humble themselves and pray and seek my face and turn from their wicked ways, then will I hear from heaven and will forgive their sin and will heal their land."*
>
> *-2 Chronicles 7:14, NIV*

Many people fail to approach God in prayer because of pride. Pride reveals itself in various ways, but the basic attitude is one that desires to live independently from any involvement of God. People might be heard to say, "I can do this on my own. I don't need God. I can find my way around this strange town, without a map, and without having to ask anyone for help!"

God wants to help you, but if you insist on independent living you will miss out on his best. God has designed you to live in dependence on him and in interdependence with one another. So let go of pride and ask God! James 4:10 says, "Humble yourselves before the Lord, and he will lift you up." God will begin to meet the needs in your life, when you take the position that your first source of help comes from God.

> In my former church, *Preston Avenue Community Church* in Saskatoon, that I served as Pastor I was always amazed at the healing services we held from time to time. Often I wondered if anyone would respond to the invitation to come and be anointed with oil for healing.

> It can be a humbling experience to rise from your seat and stand at the front of the church altar for healing. Yet people would come in faith and humility, and God did the miraculous. Time and again I saw people healed in ways that only God could accomplish.

When you do not take the first step toward God in prayer, you miss out on his blessing. Many people remain in marriages that continue to falter, because they want to work it out without God. Many people continue to be sick because they take every other avenue except God. In the Old Testament a story is told of King Asa who refused help from God for his diseased feet. In 2 Chronicles 16:12-13 it says

> In the thirty-ninth year of his reign Asa was afflicted with a disease in his feet. Though his disease was severe, even in his illness *he did not seek help from the Lord*, but only from the physicians. Then in the forty-first year of his reign *Asa died* and rested with his fathers.

I wonder how different king Asa's life could have been if he just took the time to submit his pride and ask God for help. I wonder how different our lives might be if we "let go and let God?" What type of healings would we experience in our marriages, homes, churches, workplaces, and communities if we asked God first?

It is not always easy to come to God first, because we grow accustomed to our methods, routines, and self assuredness. If it worked this way before, it should work again, and we soon leave God out of the picture.

I was reminded of this principle one time when I approached two people to share their stories of healing at our healing service. I picked up the phone and made my first call to a woman who had been healed of allergies. I knew she was interested in sharing, and so I was extremely confident that she would say yes to my request. Feeling self-assured, I phoned, but was shocked to hear she was not ready to share her story this time.

God seemed to say to me, "you do not have this testimony, because you did not ask me first." It was no fault of hers, but simply my failure to ask God. Immediately I prayed that God would prepare the heart of the next lady I wanted to ask. I prayed specifically that she would say yes to share her story of God healing her back from osteoporosis at our healing service. I then phoned and the response was an immediate yes!

Greater things can happen in your life and in your prayers as you let go of pride and first come to God for his guidance, power, and blessing. You will be amazed and glad that you did.

Overcome the Fear of Change

"Be strong and courageous. Do not be terrified; do not be discouraged, for the LORD your God will be with you wherever you go."

-Joshua 1:9b, NIV

Although change was not an issue for the man who came to his friend at midnight asking for bread, I find that some people hesitate to ask God because of the change it might bring into their lives. You may have heard the comment 'Be careful what you ask for. You might just get it!' The musical group *Caedmon's Call* sing a line in one of their songs:

> *All the time I'm thinking, wondering how would it be to breathe in deep. I guess I need to be careful when I ask for a drink (just might get what I ask for) and I know just what you'd say to me. That's why I don't ask you.*[4]

Do you hesitate in asking God for his plan for your life, because you fear change? You might know what you should ask for, but refrain because it means you will have to change your lifestyle or take on added responsibility.

- God please help me to become a true servant of you, but don't turn me into a missionary or pastor!

- God please bring healing into my marriage, but don't make me change my way of life!

- God please bless me with financial wealth, but don't ask me to give a tenth or even more of it away!

- God please give me a really good job, but don't make me take more education and training for it!

- God please bring growth to our church, but don't ask us to change the way we do things around here!

There are some results in your life that will only happen when you are willing to accept change and deal with responsibility. Until you are able to do this, you will not be able to ask God with total conviction for the things you want. Jesus' disciples could not convincingly pray for harvest workers, until they were willing to become harvest workers themselves. In Matthew 9:38 Jesus tells his disciples to "ask the Lord of the harvest, therefore, to send out workers into his harvest field." A few verses later, Matthew 10:5, it says, "these twelve Jesus sent out." They prayed. They enlisted. God worked.

> I remember the fears I felt when I began to consider a change in my last ministry setting. I sensed that God was calling me away from pastoral leadership in a smaller church and into leadership of a larger church with multiple staff. At first I wondered if I could make the transition. Could a small-church pastor move into a large-scale leadership role? Did I have what it takes? Did I have the skill-set necessary to take on a new level of leadership and responsibility?
>
> As I wrestled with the doubts in my head, God broke into my world and assured me that he would be with me. He reminded me how he took Moses, a shepherd of sheep, and transformed him into a leader of a nation. Moses survived his change and succeeded, because he did not rely

on his ability, but on God's. That day God's peace and assurance came over me and I wrote on a scrap piece of paper these words:

I may doubt my own ability, but I do not doubt God's ability. Moses went straight from being a shepherd of sheep, to being a leader of multitudes. Was he scared? Yes! Was he nervous? Yes! But these he did not rely on, but God.

And so God said to me "do not let size deter you from moving to greater levels of ministry." If God did it with Moses, he can do it with me. And so I sent out resumes to larger churches with multi-staff situations. A few months later God opened the doors for me to become part of a large church and multi-staff team at New Life Church in Stonewall, Manitoba. It has been a smooth transition and a great fit. Although I had to adapt to a new ministry setting, I have felt the support of the staff I work with and the congregation to whom I minister. God has given me strength to accomplish what he called me to, and has confirmed over and over again that he was the one who initiated this change in my life.

If God is the author of the change in your life, then he will make sure to see you through it. As such you don't need to be worried about the changes that God will bring into your life as a result of your prayers. He will always give you the strength to make it through. So if there is something you know God is calling you to pray for, go ahead and ask it of him. God does not want you to be stuck in a zone of your life that makes you miss out on his direction. Don't be afraid and back away from the future God has for you, because in God's hand everything becomes good.

GOING DEEPER

"Overcoming Barriers in Asking"

1. Of the four barriers in asking what is the most difficult for you to overcome? What are some reasons as to why this is and how can you overcome this barrier?

2. Like the "lone ship survivor" can you think of a prayer request of yours that God might be trying to answer, but in a different way than you imagine? List the ways he might do so.

3. When is it appropriate to feel guilty? When is it not appropriate to feel guilty in asking things of God?

4. What areas in your life do you try and take things into your own hands, rather than depending on God and asking him for the answers?

5. Why do you think King Asa refused to seek help from God for his diseased feet?

6. Tell of a time in your life when God answered your prayer, but it meant you changing your lifestyle or taking on added responsibility. How did you feel at first? How do feel about it now as you look back?

7. What are some of the zones you are stuck in? Can you see where God wants you? Where is it?

Setting Guidelines to Asking

"Ask the LORD for rain in the springtime."
-Zechariah 10:1, NIV

There are certain things that you can do to be more effective in asking things of God and getting a positive response. For example when I attended college and seminary I had to incorporate some of these guidelines to get an answer from the professor for the questions that were on my mind. First I needed to be clear on the nature of my query. What was the problem or dilemma that I was facing with a certain concept or text? Second I needed to ask my question promptly while it was still on my mind and in the context of discussion. If I procrastinated the opportunity passed me by because either we had moved on to a new topic, a class member beat me to another question, or the bell had rung. Third I needed to ask within the parameters of the discussion. If we were discussing the nature of the Trinity, I could not suddenly ask a question from my professor about how to change the oil in my car! It would not have been answered because it was outside the parameters of the class subject matter. In the pages to follow I want to address these three guidelines to aid you in asking things from God.

Unload Your Problems

"I pour out my problems to him; I tell him my troubles."

-Psalm 142:2, NCV

The first guideline to effectively asking God for the things in your life is to completely open up to him and reveal your desires, problems, and needs. In the parable from Luke 11:5-10 Jesus reveals that the man unloaded his problems to his friend at midnight in hopes that his friend would empathize with his dilemma and respond favourably. As the man presented his needs openly, the neighbour understood the problem and responded appropriately with bread to feed the man's travelling guest.

God is also a friend in whom you should find the freedom to unload your problems. If anyone can handle the burdens of your heart God can. Francois Fenelon, a seventeenth-century Roman Catholic Frenchman, said this about prayer:

> Tell God all that is in your heart, as one unloads one's heart, its pleasures and its pains, to a dear friend. Tell Him your troubles, that He may comfort you; tell Him your joys, that He may sober them; tell Him your longings, that He may purify them; tell Him your dislikes, that He may help you to conquer them; talk to Him of your temptations, that He may shield you from them; show Him the wounds of your heart, that He may heal them; lay bare your indifference to good, your depraved tastes for evil, your instability. Tell Him how self-love makes you unjust to others, how vanity tempts you to be insincere, how pride disguises you to yourself and others.

> If you thus pour out all your weaknesses, needs, troubles, there will be no lack of what to say. You will never exhaust the subject. It is continually being renewed. People who have no secrets from each other never want for subject of conversation. They do not weigh their words, for there is nothing to be held back; neither do they seek for something to say. They talk out of the abundance of the heart, without consideration they say just what they think. Blessed are they who attain to such familiar, unreserved intercourse with God.[5]

When I reflect on some of the old-time hymns I am reminded of their powerful words to draw near God with all that is on our heart. As a friend and Father, God is waiting to hear from us. One of these hymns, *Tell it to Jesus,* goes as such:

> Are you weary, are you heavy hearted? Tell it to Jesus. Tell it to Jesus. Are you grieving over joys departed? Tell it to Jesus alone.
>
> Do the tears flow down your cheeks unbidden? Tell it to Jesus. Tell it to Jesus. Have you sins that to men's eyes are hidden? Tell it to Jesus alone.
>
> Do you fear the gath'ring clouds of sorrow? Tell it to Jesus. Tell it to Jesus. Are you anxious what shall be tomorrow? Tell it to Jesus alone.

Are you troubled at the thought of dying? Tell it to Jesus. Tell it to Jesus. For Christ's coming Kingdom are you sighing? Tell it to Jesus alone.

Tell it to Jesus, tell it to Jesus. He is a friend that's well known; You've no other such a friend or brother. Tell it to Jesus alone.

Another hymn, *What a Friend We Have in Jesus*, was written by Joseph Scriven. It had its beginnings after a devastating tragedy. On the night before Scriven was to be married, his fiancée drowned. In his deep sorrow, Joseph realized that he could find the solace and support he needed only in his dearest friend, Jesus. Later when his mother became quite ill, he wrote the words of this hymn to comfort her. It is a hymn that reminds us of the powerful effect that unloading our heart to God in prayer can have in our lives.

What a friend we have in Jesus, all our sins and griefs to bear! What a privilege to carry everything to God in prayer! O what peace we often forfeit, O what needless pain we bear, all because we do not carry everything to God in prayer!

Have we trials and temptations? Is there trouble anywhere? We should never be discouraged, take it to the Lord in prayer. Can we find a friend so faithful who will all our sorrows share? Jesus knows our every weakness, take it to the Lord in prayer.

Are we weak and heavy laden, cumbered with a load of care? Precious Saviour, still our refuge, take it to the Lord in prayer. Do thy friends despise, forsake thee? Take it to the Lord in prayer; in His arms He'll take and shield thee, thou wilt find a solace there.

Do Not Procrastinate

"But I will call on God, and the LORD will rescue me. Morning, noon, and night I plead aloud in my distress, and the LORD hears my voice."

-Psalm 55:16-17, NLT

A second guideline to effectively ask God for the things in your life is to present your requests to him without delay. King David knew the value of approaching God immediately and throughout the day for his needs. He didn't wait until he could understand his feelings, or to try and solve his situation on his own. He came to God with the full force of his feelings and asked for help.

When I reflect on this parable that Jesus had told in relation to prayer, I wonder why the man came to his neighbour's house for help at such a late hour. Did it take a crisis situation before the man asked his friend for bread? He may have known his visiting guest was coming to his house days earlier, but never took the time to see if he had enough food on hand. He may have had the chance during that same day to go and buy some bread from the local market, but yet he procrastinated and let the situation get worse. He faced a crisis and now he needed help.

How quickly do you come to God for help? Like the man in the parable do you let your situations turn into a crisis before you ask God for help? Do you try to make it on our own?

Pride and procrastination often go hand in hand. I know that I can sometimes expend a lot of energy and waste a lot of valuable time when I fail to ask questions. Rather than phoning a store to see if an item is in stock I assume it is, go to the store and find out they are all sold out! Or if I am in a new city or section of country I think I can find my destination without asking for any directions. I drive and drive while watching the needle on my fuel gage work its way closer to empty. Finally I listen to my wife to stop the vehicle and ask directions, and then make her get out of the car to ask directions!

Procrastination can keep you from experiencing many of the good things that God has in his storeroom for you. When you fail to ask you fail to receive. You may miss that job promotion, that date with a special girl or guy, that chance to take an exotic trip, that opportunity to get involved in your church and grow in your faith, and on goes the list.

Procrastination can also harm those we seek to help. It reminds me of a story of how those closest to us suffer when we procrastinate and do something else.

> A farm boy accidentally overturned his wagon load of corn in the road. The farmer who lived nearby came to investigate. "Hey, Willis," he called out, "forget your troubles for a spell and

come on in and have dinner with us. Then I'll help you get the wagon up."

"That's mighty nice of you," Willis answered, "But I don't think Pa would like me to."

"Aw, come on, son!" the farmer insisted.

"Well, okay," the boy finally agreed. "But Pa won't like it."

After a hearty dinner, Willis thanked his host. "I feel a lot better now, but I just know Pa is going to be real upset."

"Don't be foolish!" exclaimed the neighbour. "By the way, where is he?"

"Under the wagon!"

Sometimes I can keep those closest to me under the wagon when I fail to ask God and seek the help I need. I need to ask questions to receive answers in how to be a better husband, a better father, and a better pastor. If I do not grow they may not either. My failure to ask may mean a less adequate situation for those dearest to me.

So no matter what is happening in your life remember to keep God in the centre of it all. Ask him to help you in things that are both minor and major. Don't try to figure the situation out on your own, because you might just get more muddled up and harm those closest to you. Ask now.

Stay Within God's Parameters

"So be careful to do what the LORD your God has commanded you; do not turn aside to the right or to the left. Walk in all the way that the LORD your God has commanded you, so that you may live and prosper."

-Deuteronomy 5:32-33, NIV

A third guideline in asking God for the things in your life is to identify your need and ask accordingly. In Jesus' parable on prayer the one thing this man should be commended for is that he did not go beyond what was needed at the moment. He needed bread not his friend's cattle and sheep, his house and furniture, or his money and treasured goods. He could have asked for everything and received nothing. He knew what was needed and that is what he asked for.

Be careful to not let greed take over your life. The seed for greed often begins in misdiagnosed needs. The greed to want more than what is needed at the moment is often what keeps people from experiencing the provision of God. Yes you can ask God for everything you want, but why do you make such requests? James 4:3 says, "When you ask, you do not receive, because you ask with wrong motives, that you may spend what you get on your pleasures." What is it that you need or someone else needs at this point in time?

God doesn't mind you asking him for your wants. He wants to grant you the desires of your heart. And so keep on asking him, but also be ready to not receive your desires. Sometimes God will correct your motives and other factors in your life before he will grant you the request you ask for.

Not only do motives play an important part in asking, but also the specific things you ask for. Staying within God's parameters is to ask according to God's will. 1 John 5:14-15 says "This is the confidence we have in approaching God: that if we ask anything according to his will, he hears us. And if we know that he hears us—whatever we ask—we know that we have what we asked of him."

When you receive a positive answer to a prayer request you can have confidence that this is God's will for your life (unless you have completely forced and pried open the situation or thing you wanted). Yet a prayer answered which gives you a sense of peace and satisfaction reveals that this is God's will for you. When a prayer is not answered it is then that you must trust God and believe your situation and life is still in the will of God and is being used for his purposes. Perhaps God is rerouting the direction of your life.

Some people claim, however, that every prayer of yours should be answered. It is simply a lack of faith on your part. This "name and claim it" philosophy, however, is not a guarantee success. You can believe all you want about something God will give you, but if it is outside the parameters of his will, you can believe until you are blue in the face. For example

- You can pray that God will protect you on the road, but insist on travelling over the speed limit.

- You can pray that God will help you win the lottery, but refuse to tithe the money you have now.

- You can pray that God will give you that woman, even though she is married to another man.

God wants to give you what is best. He waits for you to ask him, but he will not give you something that will harm you and others or discredit his Word.

1 John 3:22-23 says we "receive from him anything we ask, because we obey his commands and do what pleases him. And this is his command: to believe in the name of his Son, Jesus Christ, and to love one another as he commanded us." You will receive greater answers to your prayers when you fully devote your life to pleasing God and obey his commandment to believe in Jesus and love people. How well do you obey God's commands and live to please him? Do you believe in Jesus as the Son of God? Do you love certain people or all people?

GOING DEEPER

"Setting Guidelines to Asking"

1. How does God use difficulty in your life to bring you into a deeper, more open conversation with him?

2. Tell of a time when God helped you overcome a difficulty in your life.

3. List the areas in your life that overwhelm you right now and then tell them to Jesus.

4. Why do you think the man in Jesus' parable came to his friend at midnight to ask for bread?

5. What "good things" are you missing out on because you keep putting off addressing it?

6. How does prayer become a gauge for determining if you are in the centre of God's will for your life?

7. How do you discern right or wrong motives when asking God for the personal things of your life?

Finding Reasons for Asking

"Let us then approach the throne of grace with confidence, so that we may receive mercy and find grace to help us in our time of need."

-Hebrews 4:16, NIV

When I think of my days in college and seminary there were certain professors I could ask questions of more freely than others. If I could take all my professors and mould them into one super-professor there would be are four key characteristics that they would possess. One is that they would be approachable. No question would be a dumb question. I would be made to feel important and not looked down on for my lack of knowledge. Secondly they would be able to answer whatever question I had or solve whatever problem I struggled with. They would have all resources at their disposal. Thirdly I would want a professor who was aware of the subject matter I was asking. For example if I wanted to know how to preach better I would approach my homiletics professor and not my history professor. Finally I would want a professor who would be available to take questions outside of class time. When I think of reasons to ask things of God in prayer, these four traits come to mind.

God is Approachable

"Because of Christ and our faith in him, we can now come fearlessly into God's presence, assured of his glad welcome."

-Ephesians 3:12, NLT

It is because of the Father-child relationship we can have with God that allows us to approach him without fear of being reproved. His arms are held wide open for us.

I love the story of the loving father and the prodigal son in the Bible. It reveals the apprehension of the son in approaching his father, but the openness of the father in welcoming back a son who rejected him, ran away, and spent all his inheritance in wild living. In Luke 15:17-24 we read

> When he came to his senses, he said, 'How many of my father's hired men have food to spare, and here I am starving to death! I will set out and go back to my father and say to him: Father, I have sinned against heaven and against you. I am no longer worthy to be called your son; make me like one of your hired men.' So he got up and went to his father.
>
> But while he was still a long way off, his father saw him and was filled with compassion for him; he ran to his son, threw his arms around him and kissed him.
>
> The son said to him, 'Father, I have sinned against heaven and against you. I am no longer worthy to be called your son.'
>
> But the father said to his servants, 'Quick! Bring the best robe and put it on him. Put a ring on his finger and sandals on his feet. Bring the fattened calf and kill it. Let's have a feast and celebrate.

> For this son of mine was dead and is alive again; he was lost and is found.' So they began to celebrate.

Rather than reproving the son for his actions this loving father fully accepted him back. Before the run-away son could finish his sentence about wanting to be treated like one of the hired men, the father quickly got him the best robe, a gesture of honour. He put a ring, a sign of authority, and put it on his finger. He brought him sandals, a symbol of acceptance, and placed them on his feet. Servants in those days went around in bare feet. He also held a great feast for his son, a sign of great joy, for the son that was lost was now found.

Although not every earthly parent models this character of openness most do for their children. They are approachable, even when their children have messed up. I think of my own parents. I do not have to fear that they will turn me away because of the questions I have or the help that I need. Although they might not be able to answer every question or help me in every need they remain approachable and do their best.

God who is the perfect parent is always approachable. Ask him what you will. Jesus said in John 6:37b "whoever comes to me I will never drive away." You should feel confident and at ease to approach God with whatever is on your heart. Do not hold back from God because you have grown up with the erroneous idea that every time you come near God he wants to remind you of your sin, punish you for your actions, and reject you because you are unworthy. The truth is that God has made you in his image and loves you. Like the father of the prodigal son he waits with a longing heart for you to come to him. And when you do he will put on a great feast for you as well.

God is Able

"What is impossible from a human perspective is possible with God."

-Luke 18:27, NLT

I have seen many miracles in my life. One such time was when my cousins and I were driving back late at night from a wedding. After the reception we quickly jumped in the car and started driving with no thought about looking at the gas gauge. About a half hour later we noticed the gas tank was on empty, but hoped to make it to the next town to fill up. Unfortunately no station was open and so we decided to proceed to the next town—again with no luck. Driving on fumes and with about 150 kilometres to our destination we began to wonder how much farther we could make it.

Passing town after town with no station open, worry mounting and hope disappearing, we finally came to a truck-stop town that we felt certain would have a gas station open. To our shock every station was closed!

It was at that moment in the back seat of the car that I quietly asked God to perform the impossible and help us reach our destination,

> which was still 75 kilometres away! In complete astonishment we kept driving, passing town after town, until we reached our destination—the city of Regina, Saskatchewan.
>
> I thanked God for this incredible answer to prayer and then we quickly found the nearest gas station and filled the car to overflowing! That evening late at night God showed us his amazing power and his ability to accomplish the impossible.

Another reason you should ask God to meet the needs of your life is that he is all-powerful or omnipotent. Nothing is impossible for God to accomplish. Every resource is at his disposal. What is it that you need? What are the things in your life that you think you will never receive? God is more than able to answer your prayers. Ephesians 3:20 says "Now to him who is able to do immeasurably more than all we ask or imagine, according to his power that is at work within us." And so ask God for the big things in your life. If anyone can bring about the results that you desire God can!

There is a story in the Bible about two blind men who had to rely on the powerful ability of Jesus to heal them. Although from a human perspective they could see no cure for their blindness they heard about the miraculous powers of Jesus. One day as Jesus passed their way they shouted to Jesus in anticipation that he would heal them. In Matthew 9:27-30 it says

> As Jesus went on from there, two blind men followed him, calling out, "Have mercy on us, Son of David!"
>
> When he had gone indoors, the blind men came to him, and he asked them, "Do you believe that I am able to do this?"
>
> "Yes, Lord," they replied.
>
> Then he touched their eyes and said, "According to your faith will it be done to you"; and their sight was restored.

Although you might not be physically blind like these two men you may be tempted to settle for hopeless situations in your life because you are blinded with despair. From a human perspective what are the things you feel will never change in your life or in the lives of those around you? Now is the time to approach Jesus with anticipation of what he can do in your life. Follow him and cry out for his mercy and compassion. He has the power to meet your needs.

> In my current ministry I have seen God's amazing ability to do the impossible: When I first started my new position as an associate pastor at New Life Church part of my role was in dealing with the administration of the church. I came in August 2007 and by September the church finances were behind by $23, 000. Not good for just arriving on the scene! This was a sizable chunk of money.

To address this situation I met with my finance committee a number of times. As we looked at the numbers and trends we projected a substantial deficit at year-end. We made plans to cut back the budget for 2008 something we hoped not to do. Letters were sent to each of the ministry leaders to be cautious and limit their spending to only necessary items.

It was unsettling to know we were this far behind in the budget, but with the prompting of the Senior Pastor we began to make this a matter of serious prayer. In our weekly staff meetings and monthly board meetings we prayed that God would "meet and exceed our budget."

It was amazing to see God unleash his power and provision in our midst. Week after week we saw the financial figures continue to get better. Finally by the end of the year rather than ending with a huge deficit we finished strong with a $31, 000 surplus! Rather than cutting back our budget for 2008 we increased it believing God would continue to provide and use this local ministry for his glory.

God continued to bless and by mid-summer 2008 we were $21, 000 ahead of our increased budget. Amazingly we ended the year in 2008 with a $65, 000 surplus, something our Senior Pastor, Henry Ozirney, says he had never seen in all his 38 years of ministry in the church! God gives beyond what we can even ask or imagine!

God is Aware

"Your Father knows what you need before you ask him."

-Matthew 6:8b, NIV

A third reason why you should have confidence in asking God for the things in your life is that he is all-knowing or omniscient. God is aware of every external detail of your life right down to the number of hairs on your head. For some of you that is easier to count than others!

A few months ago I was going through my personal library and I came across a book that was over 100 years old! It was titled *George Muller of Bristol and His Witness to a Prayer-Hearing God.* I read through this biography of George Muller's life (1805-1898) and the amazing ways in which God provided for his needs and that of his orphanage in England. This man displayed such confidence in prayer, because he knew God was aware of his needs.

Once when the orphanage had virtually no funds to meet the needs of hundreds of orphans a man came to inquire about the present state of the orphanage. He wanted to know exactly how much was needed and then give money toward the need. It seemed like a miracle sent from God, but George Muller decided to not make known the exact needs. He believed it would risk turning his eyes away from God and onto man, and would turn away the believer from totally depending on God. And so he prayed and trusted God.

As soon as the man left Mr. Muller sent his appeal to the living God:

> "Lord, thou knowest that, for Thy sake, I did not tell this brother about our need. Now, Lord, show afresh that there is *reality* in speaking to Thee only, about our need, and speak therefore to this brother so that he may help us."[6]

In answer to this prayer God moved the hand of this inquiring man to send one hundred pounds which came when not one penny was in hand. George Muller was a man of prayer who trusted in God's care for his life and ministry.

In his awareness God responds to the needs of your life, but he also may withhold certain things because he sees your future while you do not.

When I think of this aspect of God's nature I am compelled to rely on him. It is in God's awareness of the events that surround my life that urges me to trust him in times when I may not understand the things I go through. I am not aware of every single detail and how it affects my life, but God is. He knows why my prayers should be answered or not answered. Some situations that I think would do me good may in the weeks, months, or even years to come prove to be my downfall. Not every prayer of mine is answered in the way I think it should be, but I am learning to be content in that because God knows why.

Not every prayer of yours will be answered either, but trust God because he knows what is best for you (or that other person or organization). And so ask God for the things that surround your life, but be willing to accept the outcome. Jesus asked to be spared the cross, but God the Father knew that it was not in the best interests of humanity. Without his sacrificial death on the cross, all humanity would have been lost in their sin and forever without hope. Jesus asked, but he accepted the answer and endured the cross so that all people would have the chance to be free from sin to live with God for eternity.

God is also aware of every internal detail of your life, from the desires you crave to the hurts you bottle up. If God knows all about you why not ask him for the things on your heart? God can answer any question you have. He can solve any problem you encounter. He can understand anything you go through. Hebrews 2:18 says "because [Jesus] himself suffered when he was tempted, he is able to help those who are being tempted." It was because Jesus was human that he also understands everything you go through.

God is Available

> *"As I was with Moses, so I will be with you; I will never leave you nor forsake you."*
>
> *-Joshua 1:5, NIV*

Joshua had just experienced the loss of a great mentor and leader of Israel—Moses. Now it was up to him to lead the Israelites past the barriers and into the Promised Land. I can imagine Joshua's doubt about accomplishing this mission: "Do I have what it takes to lead Israel to the new land? Is God going to guide me just like he did Moses? Will God abandon me?"

God assured Joshua that just as he was with Moses so would he be with him. He would never leave Joshua nor forsake him. God would always be available. And so a fourth reason why you should feel confident to ask God for anything is that he will always be with you to guide you.

The Internet is widely used today because anything you want to know is at your fingertips. Type in "Wikipedia" and you will find a database filled with a wealth of information. The information you seek is online all the time. It's available 24/7 unless your computer crashes, the power goes out, or your server is down.

Like the Internet God is online all the time for you; unlike the Internet he will never crash, power out, or go down. Psalm 21:3b-4, 7b-8 says, "[God] who watches over you will not slumber; indeed, he who watches over Israel will neither slumber nor sleep...he will watch over your life; the Lord will watch over your coming and going both now and forevermore." Jesus said in Matthew 28:20b "I am with you always, to the very end of the age." You can come to God 24 hours a day, 7 days a week, 365 days a year—forever! God will never say your request is outside his working hours! His time is your time.

GOING DEEPER

"Finding Reasons for Asking"

1. Name someone who is approachable. What is it about this person that makes it easy for you to approach them?

2. In what ways is God like the father in the story of the prodigal son? How is he like that with you?

3. Tell of a time in your life when God answered a prayer of yours in an amazing way?

4. What impossible situation do you face in your life at this moment? Take time to pray about it.

5. How can an understanding of God's awareness about the external and internal details of your life help you be more patient in unanswered prayer?

6. In what ways is God like and unlike the Internet?

7. From the list of four reasons in coming to God in prayer which one do you need to become more confident in?

FIND YOUR SOLUTIONS THROUGH SEEKING

God has an answer for your requests, but he wants you to be active in working alongside him. Asking is the first step in the process of effective prayer, but you cannot just sit on your duff and expect a package from heaven to fall on your lap. You cannot simply ask God for a job and then sit watching TV all day in your house! You must move to the next step of seeking in the process of effective prayer.

I have had times in my life where God has answered my prayer after step one in this process. The same might be true for you at times. There is no need to seek out any solution. I remember a prayer request I made to God in my former church in Saskatoon and how God quickly answered this specific request.

> It was in the bleak of winter that my church experienced a dry spell in terms of visitors who came and stayed. A few visitors came, but none returned. Near the end of February I felt prompted by God to pray specifically for 10 new families to become part of the church fellowship in that year. At the monthly prayer night I encouraged the people to pray specifically for this goal to be reached. I also asked the people in my small group to pray for this request.
>
> Ten days after that prayer night God brought into our worship service two new ladies. The following week they came back with three more people and mentioned that there were others they intended to invite. About a month later another family entered our church fellowship. It was a joyous time because God was bringing people

> into the church as a result of our asking him. Within just over a month we had four different households coming to the church simply in response to that prayer!
>
> Four households were great, but the prayer was only partially fulfilled. We believed God wanted 10 families to enter the church fellowship that year. Rather than waiting passively for people to come, we began to work alongside God in seeking people. We held outreach events, advertised on our signboard, invited people to various events, and did other things to connect with people in the community. It was amazing because by the end of that year six more families joined our fellowship! God answered our prayer for 10 households to connect with our church fellowship and stay. We worked alongside God in the process of prayer.

Too often in prayer it is easy to wait for God to respond without taking any action. Unfortunately this approach may cause you to miss many of God's blessings for your life. Your desires might go unmet because this second step in the process of prayer is not pursued. There is so much that God wants to give you that is far beyond his initial blessings.

When your need is not met initially God challenges you to find the solutions through seeking. Many answers to your prayers will be found as you move ahead in action-oriented prayer. In seeking out answers to your requests there are three things that you must do to have better success.

Seek with Common Sense

> *"Do not conform any longer to the pattern of this world, but be transformed by the renewing of your mind. Then you will be able to test and approve what God's will is—his good, pleasing and perfect will."*
>
> *-Romans 12:2, NIV*

> In 1937 architect Frank Lloyd Wright built a house for industrialist Hibbard Johnson. One rainy evening Johnson was entertaining distinguished guests for dinner when the roof began to leak. The water seeped through directly above Johnson himself, dripping steadily onto his bald head. Irate, he called Wright in Phoenix, Arizona. "Frank," he said, "you built this beautiful house for me and we enjoy it very much. But I have told you the roof leaks, and right now I am with some friends and distinguished guests and it is leaking right on top of my head." Wright's reply was heard by all of the guests. "Well, Hib, why don't you move your chair?"[7]

The dictionary defines common sense as "practical intelligence." Common sense is the ability to use your intelligence to find the most practical and simplistic solution to your needs. Too often, however, people look for complex ways and systems to solve their dilemmas. Below are some examples of how to use common sense.

- To avoid being stranded on a highway with a flat tire it is common sense to have a spare tire, filled with air, stored in the vehicle.

- To avoid taking in water when diving it is common sense to close the mouth.

- To safeguard your retirement fund it is common sense to diversify your investments. As the saying goes don't put all your eggs in one basket just in case that basket breaks and the eggs fall out.

- A news clip appeared in the papers after an electricity blackout: "During the power failure many people complained of having gotten stuck for hours on escalators."[8] Common sense says use your legs when the escalator breaks down!

God has given you a brain and wants you to use it. Prayer is not always a mystical experience, but also a practical experience. Many times the solution to your prayers can be met through using common sense. When seeking God for the solution to your needs there are some practical, common sense things you can do.

Expand Your Chances of Success

> *"Remember this: Whoever sows sparingly will also reap sparingly, and whoever sows generously will also reap generously."*
>
> *-2 Corinthians 9:6, NIV*

What are the needs in your life that you seek? Sometimes the needs in your life will only be met as you expand your base of possibilities. As you expand this base the ratio of probability in receiving what you desire increases.

For example if I want to harvest 100 carrots in a home garden I may need to plant twice as many seeds to get that type of return. Some seed for various reasons may not sprout. To reap abundantly I must sow generously. The chance of success becomes greater with the more I put out. Luke 6:38 addresses this principle of sowing and reaping. It says to "give, and it will be given to you. A good measure, pressed down, shaken together and running over, will be poured into your lap. *For with the measure you use, it will be measured to you.*"

- If you need a job the more resumes you send out will give you a greater chance of getting one.

- If you need to pass an exam the more you study for it will increase your likelihood of passing.

- If you want to lose weight your chances of reaching your goal increases as you exercise more frequently and eat healthy more consistently.

- If you want a date that leads to a mate do not give up after the first rejection, but expand the possibility of people you can ask.

I remember as a young adult my strong desire to get married. Yet the dating scene was not always easy. I had my share of rejections as most guys usually do. Sometimes it was discouraging, but I believed that of all the single women in the world God must have at least one for me! And so I would think of girls I knew that might be potential lifelong partners and then ask them on a date. Now don't get me wrong. I was not so desperate that I wanted to date anyone. I was just a boy wanting to meet a girl. And then it happened. After years of seeking I met my girl.

I had to return to my former apartment complex to give my final payment. As I drove up in my fancy, four-door, rusted out, red car (not an ideal babe magnet!) I saw this beautiful blond haired girl standing by her car with the snow gently falling on her hair. In a moment of exhilaration I blurted out to God "Hey God I sure would like to meet a girl like that!"

As I walked into the apartment complex I couldn't keep my eyes off her! She was captivating! She likely thought, "Who is this creepy guy that keeps staring at me?" Inside I tried to settle accounts as fast as I could with the landlady so I could see this girl again. Well by the time I came out she was gone and I thought that was the end of that.

The next week I went with my cousin to his church for the evening service. As the pastor asked people to shake hands with others this girl in front of me turned around. We both looked at each other with stunned expressions, wondering where we had seen each other before. Well we got talking and to my amazement it was the same girl whom I could not keep my eyes off the week earlier. Not only that, but I found out she lived in the same apartment complex that I had formerly lived in. Somehow I missed connecting with her all the time I lived there.

Well from that moment it spurred me on to join my cousin every Sunday evening to attend his church service! I connected with the college age group and would often go to restaurants after the service. Finally one day I built up enough courage to ask this girl Marcy on a date and the rest is history. A year and a half later we were married and now we have three wonderful children.

God has a solution to your needs. Sometimes you must try many doors before the right one will open for you. Sometimes it may take many years before the right moment comes.

Look in Appropriate Places

"Still other seed fell on good soil. It came up and yielded a crop, a hundred times more than was sown."

-Luke 8:8, NIV

In the parable of "The Sower" Jesus gives a great analogy on how to reach greater yields.[9] The farmer who scatters seed on a hard path, rocky ground, or weedy soil will see limited results. Yet the farmer who sows in appropriate places—the good soil—will see incredible yields.

The second truth in finding better results to your prayers is that you need to seek the solution in appropriate places. The more you sow is not always the better if you sow in places that will not address your need. If my family needs food I don't go to an electronic store. I go to the grocery mart where these needs can be found.

Sowing generously means that you need to find the places where your efforts will reach their maximum return. A farmer might plant a lot of seed, but if it is sown on the road and not the cultivated field the rate of return will be nominal, if not nil, since the conditions do not fit the normal parameters. Hard work is not always a guarantee of success, but smart work coupled with hard work will bring success.

In the parable from the gospel of Luke we find how the man who needed bread finally came to his senses. He knew what he needed and he knew where he was going to find it. He did not wander outside at midnight to find bread in his sheep pen! He believed his friend's house would be the most practical place to find bread.

The reason Jesus had great success in reaching lost people is that he didn't come to observe and study about lost people, he came to "seek and to save people who are lost."[10] When you have desires and needs in your life God wants you to make the effort to seek out solutions to these needs in appropriate places.

Jesus had an impact in the lives of lost people because not only did he sow generously, but he went to places where they were. He didn't avoid them, but became known as "a friend of tax collectors and sinners."[11] In another place Jesus said, "I have not come to call the righteous, but sinners."[12] Jesus spent time with people who needed God. Some disdained Jesus' approach, but the results are proof of his wisdom and common sense.

Write out the needs in your life, family, church, or community and then in a column next to it write out the potential places or ways in which this need can be met. You will improve the chances of meeting the needs in your life as you seek these desires in the appropriate places.

- If you want to have a friend then you need to frequent places where a friendship can start.

- If you want to win people to Christ then you need to regularly hang out with non-Christians and non-churched individuals.

- If you want to promote your business then you need to constantly advertise in places where people will see it.

GOING DEEPER

"Seek with Common Sense"

1. How would you define common sense and what are some examples that you can list?

2. Think of a need in your life and then list a number of ways in which this need could be met?

3. How does increasing your base of possibilities give you greater chances to see your need met?

4. Tell of a time in your life where it took more than one attempt to realize a desire of yours?

5. What things did Jesus do to bring about such success in reaching lost people for God?

6. Think of a need and then list the places where you could go to have this need met?

7. How did the man in the parable seeking bread display or not display common sense?

Seek with Determination

"You will seek me and find me when you seek me with all your heart."

-Jeremiah 29:13, NIV

Two frogs fell into a deep cream bowl;
The one was wise, and a cheery soul.
The other one took a gloomy view
And bade his friend a sad adieu.
Said the other frog with a merry grin,
"I can't get out, but I won't give in;
I'll swim around till my strength is spent,
Then I will die the more content."
And as he swam, though ever it seemed,
His struggling began to churn the cream
Until on top of pure butter he stopped,
And out of the bowl he quickly hopped.
The moral, you ask? Oh, it's easily found!
If you can't get out, keep swimming around.

This humorous poem conveys the lesson that you should never give up on the desires of your heart, unless God reveals to you otherwise that you should. Instead the unanswered prayers in your life should motivate you to keep seeking a solution to the needs you face and the requests you make.

In the parable we have been focusing on throughout this book the man could have given up and gone home after the owner said the doors are locked and his children are in bed. Yet because of the man's determination the neighbour got out of bed and gave him what he needed.

One reason many people fail to find positive results in their requests to God is that they give up too soon. Another reason is that there is not a strong desire or pull to see this request met. Little effort is put into the seeking part of prayer. Where there is little desire there is little determination. Where there is much desire there is much determination. Someone once said "Where there's a will there's a way." Those who want something badly enough will find a way to obtain it. Of course this does not mean doing something illegal or unethical to get what you want. Your request might be granted in this way, but it doesn't come from God.

It is better to wait on God for your needs to be met than to force the situation and get what you want. God has placed desires in your life, but he knows best when and how they should be met. To wait, however, does not mean to be passive and do nothing. God calls you to keep seeking, but in a way that does not violate his standards or intentions for your life. Sometimes it is in waiting, which can be difficult at times, that God refines and sharpens your character. James 1:3-4 says "you know that the testing of your faith develops perseverance. Perseverance must finish its work so that you may be mature and complete, not lacking anything" (NIV).

A story is told in Matthew 15:21-28 about a woman whose determination and great faith produced the results she was looking for.

> 21 Leaving that place, Jesus withdrew to the
> region of Tyre and Sidon. 22 A Canaanite woman
> from that vicinity came to him, crying out,

> "Lord, Son of David, have mercy on me! My daughter is suffering terribly from demon-possession."
>
> [23]Jesus did not answer a word. So his disciples came to him and urged him, "Send her away, for she keeps crying out after us."
>
> [24]He answered, "I was sent only to the lost sheep of Israel."
>
> [25]The woman came and knelt before him. "Lord, help me!" she said.
>
> [26]He replied, "It is not right to take the children's bread and toss it to their dogs."
>
> [27]"Yes, Lord," she said, "but even the dogs eat the crumbs that fall from their masters' table."
>
> [28]Then Jesus answered, "Woman, you have great faith! Your request is granted." And her daughter was healed from that very hour.

At first glance you might be shocked at the callous remarks of Jesus to this woman. Written words, however, do not always capture tone of voice. Jesus' response to this woman was more likely to be humorous than callous. He used a satirical technique to banter with this witty woman. Jesus was not trying to get rid of her, as the disciples wanted, but to draw out her faith through his remarks. There are three things from this passage that reveal how you should seek the solutions to your requests with determination.

Determination Begins with Desire

"May he give you the desire of your heart and make all your plans succeed."

-Psalm 20:4, NIV

In the Hebrew way of thinking the heart was believed to be the place of emotion and passion in a person's life. It was the centre from which sprang one's desires. How much do you desire the thing you want? Is it coming from deep within you, or is being motivated by something or someone else? Does what you desire seem like a matter of life and death? Is it something that grips your heart so much that you cannot stop thinking about it or looking until you have found it? In Jeremiah 29:13 God said "You will seek me and find me when you seek me with *all your heart*."

This Canaanite woman was moved deep within her heart for her daughter. Nothing could stop her from seeking Jesus who had the power to release her daughter from demon-possession. Desire precedes determination for without it we would give up at the first sign of hardship or failure.

When I took my master's degree through Prairie Graduate School in Calgary, Alberta I had countless books and articles to read, assignments to complete, and papers to write. At times it was tough slugging, but my desire to earn this degree kept me going and in time I graduated. Desire prompts determination. The farmer keeps going despite harsh conditions, because he or she is motivated by the end goal of a bumper crop. The parent does not give up training their child at the first sign of immaturity, but continues because of their desire to see a fully mature adult. What you truly desire will be what you truly seek.

It was the desire for humanity's redemption that motivated Jesus to overcome the deterrent of crucifixion on the cross. He loved you and me so much that he came to this world so that we might not perish but have eternal life. Jesus would never have put up with ridicule, insults, and ultimate crucifixion if he had no desire to bring you and me back into a relationship with God his Father. Hebrews 12:2-3 says

> Let us look only to Jesus, the One who began our faith and who makes it perfect. He suffered death on the cross. But he accepted the shame as if it were nothing because of the joy that God put before him. And now he is sitting at the right side of God's throne. Think about Jesus' example. He held on while wicked people were doing evil things to him. So do not get tired and stop trying. (NCV)

Are you losing heart because what you desire has not come about? Keep going, because what you seek, if it is according to God's purpose, will be found. Ask God to fill you with his desires and give you the strength to continue with determination.

Determination Perseveres Through Silence

> *"O LORD, you have seen this; be not silent. Do not be far from me, O Lord."*
>
> *-Psalm 35:22, NIV*

One of the hardest things in this age of instant information is the silence of God to our requests. Our thoughts might range from "does God not hear?" to "does God not care?" In our day when something does not come by quickly we often give up and move on to something or someone else. W. Bingham Hunter says in his book *The God Who Hears:*

> If you want to trust God for more than instant answers, you may have to change the way you live. It's hard, very hard, for Christians who are used to instant pudding, instant credit and instant replay to wait for anything...even God."[13]

Jesus told the disciples that they would receive the Holy Spirit when he left this world. Yet it did not happen immediately. It took 10 long days of earnest prayer to God before the Holy Spirit was given to the disciples. Seek with determination, even in the silence of God, and you will eventually find God's blessing.

This Canaanite woman had to change her thinking process to find God's blessing. At first she might have been taken aback by Jesus' refusal to respond immediately to her plea for help. She may have wondered why Jesus was not responding to the legitimate need for deliverance in her daughter's life. Yet silence was not an option. Rather than giving up in her desire to see her daughter healed she kept pursuing Jesus because he held the solution to her request.

You may be wondering why Jesus ignored this woman's request. To me Jesus was not being callous, but calculating. He knew what it would take for this woman to truly respond to him. In his seemingly silence, he used a technique to test the sincerity of this woman's plea. He wanted to draw out and deepen her faith. Sometimes things that come by easily are easily forgotten; things that come by with difficulty are forever remembered. In this test of faith Jesus was giving her an experience and lesson that she would remember for a lifetime.

I remember in my teen years the silence of God in a request for physical healing from acne lesions. They were painful, humiliating, and no fun to have. For six years I asked God to remove these lesions from me but to no avail. God seemed distant; he seemed silent. I questioned whether he was a God of love or a God of hate. Why would he let me go through this ordeal? Finally when I hit my young adult years the problem cleared up and I thanked God for this, but I always wondered why it took so long for him to respond. Why did I have to put up with that pain for six years?

Twenty years later God finally revealed his answer to me. A few summers ago I was sitting in a restaurant with two of my colleagues from work. We were discussing our childhood experiences and asked if anyone ever rebelled against their parents or strayed from the faith. We each had different hurts we experienced as teenagers, but it did not cause us to rebel against our parents or God. In that moment God shone a light into my heart and I understood.

> It was in my pain that God protected me. He set me on a path toward him that I may never have chosen. It was in my pain and humiliation that I withdrew from my peers and others. In that choice of seclusion God protected me by leading me not into temptation, but delivering me from evil. My seclusion kept me from joining my peers in doing things that might discredit my faith, integrity, and God's future plans for me as a pastor. Sometimes your pain is God's way of protecting you from a path that may lead you away and not nearer to him.

It is in times of silence and waiting that God tests you to see if you really want what you desire. God rewards those who seek him diligently. Hebrews 11:6 says "Without faith it is impossible to please God, because anyone who comes to him must believe that he exists and that he rewards those who earnestly seek him."

If you keep seeking to meet a certain need in your life it is most likely that you will be responsible, grateful, and careful when the need is met. Handouts are often abused and can create thankless individuals. Hard work for something ensures responsibility and gratefulness when it is received.

Like this Canaanite woman when your cry is not heard at once continue to follow Jesus and keep looking to find the solution to your needs. Great faith does not give up in the face of silence, but perseveres through it.

Determination Overcomes Setback

"In this world you will have trouble. But take heart! I have overcome the world."

-John 16:33, NIV

Jesus could have easily given up with the obstacles that he faced in his ministry. The Jewish leaders plotted to kill him, his hometown didn't believe him, his siblings rejected his claims, his close friend and disciple Peter denied knowing him and another disciple Judas Iscariot betrayed him. If anyone had trouble Jesus did and yet in faith he pressed on because he was determined to obey his Father's will and become the Saviour of all humanity. Even the grave could not hold him down. Through his resurrection he overcame the greatest of all setbacks—death. In that we have been given hope and a future to press on despite what we face now. The Apostle Paul writes in Romans 8:35-39

> Who shall separate us from the love of Christ? Shall trouble or hardship or persecution or famine or nakedness or danger or sword? As it is written:
>
>> "For your sake we face death all day long; we are considered as sheep to be slaughtered."
>
> No, in all these things we are more than conquerors through him who loved us. For I am convinced that neither death nor life, neither angels nor demons, neither the present nor the

future, nor any powers, neither height nor depth, nor anything else in all creation, will be able to separate us from the love of God that is in Christ Jesus our Lord. (NIV)

Any time you are setback God is setting you up for a comeback. This Canaanite woman did not give up for her daughter's spiritual and emotional health the first time she experienced a setback, but she continued on. Jesus' remarks to this woman might seem like a possible setback for some people, but to this woman she kept her wits and impressed Jesus with her persevering faith. His remarks were not meant to dissuade her, but to challenge her to a greater faith. In seeing results to her request she had to overcome two areas of possible setback:

Setback in priority: Jesus states that his mission was to the Jews and not to the Gentiles. Jesus had to be exclusive in order to be effective. If he did not start somewhere the mission would go nowhere. Yet Jesus was not so rigid in his mission to the Jews that he refused to help the Gentiles. One day his mission would be global as his disciples took the gospel to all nations to make disciples of all people. If Jesus was unbending he would have outright refused the request of this woman. And so the woman kept pursuing Jesus and did not recoil at his comment for she believed in Jesus' love for all people.

Setback in Blessing: In talking with this woman Jesus says it is not right to give what is intended for the Jews to the Gentiles. Again we must see these comments in light of a comical situation. Max Lucado writes

> He knows he can heal her daughter. He knows he isn't bound by a plan. He knows her heart is good. So he decides to engage in a humourous moment with a faithful woman. In essence, here's what they said:
>
> "Now, you know God only cares about Jews," he says smiling.
>
> And when she catches on, she volleys back, "But your bread is so precious, I'll be happy to eat the crumbs."
>
> In a spirit of exuberance, he bursts out, "Never have I seen such faith! Your daughter is healed."
>
> This story does not portray a contemptuous God. It portrays a willing One who delights in a sincere seeker.[14]

There are times when you might want to give up on finding solutions to the needs in your life because of the insurmountable setbacks you experience. Yet if you keep seeking you will eventually find. The Canaanite woman overcame this setback of blessing, because she knew God was generous to all. His sun and rain are given to the just and unjust alike.

What was an apparent setback was overcome through persuasive arguments and deep faith in the power of Jesus. In her banter with Jesus this Canaanite women used a technique of prayer that is not readily used in our day. It was a technique of prayer used in the lives of Old Testament patriarchs and of the modern day

George Muller. In the biography of *George Muller of Bristol and His Witness to the Prayer-Hearing God*, Pierson writes of this man of faith and prayer:

> This man who had determined to risk everything upon God's word of promise, turned from doubtful devices and questionable methods of relief to *pleading with God.* And it may be well to mark his *manner* of pleading. He used *argument* in prayer.
>
> This method of *holy argument*—ordering our cause before God, as an advocate would plead before a judge—is not only almost a lost art, but to many it actually seems almost puerile. And yet it is abundantly taught and exemplified in Scripture. Abraham in his plea for Sodom is the first great example of it. Moses excelled in this art, in many crises interceding in behalf of the people with consummate skill, marshalling arguments as a general-in-chief marshals batallions. Elijah on Carmel is a striking example of power in this special pleading.
>
> Of course God does not *need to be convinced:* no arguments can make any plainer to Him the claims of trusting souls to His intervention, claims based upon His own word, confirmed by His oath. And yet He will be inquired of and argued with. That is His way of blessing. He loves to have us set before Him our cause and His own promises: He delights in the well-ordered plea, where argument is piled upon argument.[15]

After reading this section in this biography on George Muller I recall in the spring of 2009 praying in this style. I knew the thing I wanted was not in God's specific will, it was just something I wanted to see happen. Let me explain:

> One of my favourite hockey teams in the NHL is the Pittsburgh Penguins and they made it to the Stanley Cup finals. I was excited to see this happen, but after game two the team was down 2-0 and not looking good. I said to God "I know a certain team winning is not in your direct will, but as a Father you do like to see your children happy. I know it doesn't matter who really wins, because in 10 years from now I won't remember much if anything of this series. I come asking you to help Pittsburgh win the Stanley Cup because you delight in blessing your children." I left it at that and was content in whichever way the series went.
>
> Well the next two games the Penguins won and the series was tied up. Then the Detroit Red Wings won game five and were one win away from the Cup. I couldn't see game six because I was away helping at a camp for my daughter, but I sure hoped Pittsburgh would win so I could be back and see game seven. Again I appealed to God's nature of blessing his children for no other reason than to make them happy. Well sure enough they won! I made sure everything else was cleared off my calendar for game seven of the Stanley Cup—a game that is always exciting. The Penguins would be playing in the home

arena of the Red Wings a tough feat to win since they lost all three games in that arena. But I kept my hope alive in the nature of God and reminded God of my prayer.

The game began and the Penguins took a 2-0 lead, but then the Red Wings began to come back. They scored a goal, and were pressing hard at the end of third period to tie it up. With six seconds left to go in the game, a flurry of shots was fired on the Pittsburgh goaltender Marc Andre Fleury. With the dying seconds one shot was about to go in, but in the last moment Fleury lunged and fell sideways stopping the shot. The Penguins held on to win the Stanley Cup!

It was an exciting moment to capture, but more than that I extremely grateful for having a God who delights in blessing his children. I may not remember the series in 10-20 years from now, but I will remember this moment of blessing from God and the way in which appealing to his nature in prayer can bring about desired results.

GOING DEEPER

"Seek with Determination"

1. In what ways is desire connected with determination in prayer?

2. In what ways did the Canaanite woman show determination to see her daughter healed?

3. Tell of a time where you had to wait a long time before seeing a prayer answered? Is there any prayer you are still waiting on God to answer?

4. What reasons do you think Jesus had in not responding immediately to the request of this Canaanite woman?

5. How do you respond when God seems silent in answering your prayer requests?

6. What situation in your life do you feel setback in? How can prayer help you overcome this setback?

7. Where in your life do you need to appeal to God's nature and plead for him to meet your needs?

Seek in Partnership

"Two people are better than one, because they get more done by working together."

-Ecclesiastes 4:9, NCV

The kindergarten Sunday school class was learning about how God cares for us in times of trouble. The teacher asked the class to draw pictures of things that make them afraid. After they finished drawing, each child explained to the others what he or she had drawn.

Five-year-old Scott had created in vivid crayon a looming funnel cloud, a car, and a man. He described how the man could not get his car started and a tornado was coming toward him.

"The man really needs to pray, doesn't he?" asked the teacher.

"No," Scott disagreed. "He needs to run!"[16]

Someone once said, "God helps those who help themselves." There is a time to pray, but there is also a time for action. Prayer is not a passive, inactive ritual to make a Christian appear more holy. Prayer is an active response in working alongside God to meet the daily needs and conditions around you. Martin Luther once said, "Pray as if everything depends on God, then work as if everything depends on you." Prayer is a partnership with God. God will do his part as long as you do your part. Prayer is actively working alongside God in meeting your needs.

- When Jesus called his first disciples he did not hope through osmosis that they would know he wanted them. He went down by the lakeside, the tax collector's booth, and other places and said to those standing there "Come follow me."

- When Jesus prayed for his team of apostles he did not wait until his disciples came to him to volunteer, but rather he went to them and selected them. Alongside God his Father he was active in the process of selection.

- The person who is hungry and asks God for food will likely starve if no action is involved. The Bible says "if a man will not work, he shall not eat."[17]

- The person who sits on the couch waiting for a job to fall into their lap is like a person who plays the lottery. The odds are not in their favour!

- The church that wants people to follow Jesus and attend church need to be active in finding non-Christian and non-churched individuals.

God has a solution to your needs, but you need to be active in finding it. Many needs are only met as you learn to work alongside God and others in the process. Paul says in 1 Corinthians 3:5-6, 9a "Through us God caused you to believe. Each of us did the work the Lord gave us. My job was to plant the seed in your hearts, and Apollos watered it, but it was God, not we, who made it grow…we work together as partners who belong to God" (NLT).

Philip Yancey in his book, *Prayer: Does it Make Any Difference?,* has a chapter on "Partnership." In it he writes…

> From the very beginning God has relied on human partners to advance the process of creation. After equipping Adam to cultivate the land and supervise the animals, God left the work of the garden in his hands…When God wanted a dwelling place on earth, a tabernacle and temple did not descend from the sky like a spaceship; thousands of artists and craftsmen worked to fashion them…Jesus himself had appealed to the Lord of the harvest, in an all-night ordeal that resulted in the twelve disciples standing before him. Now he called on those twelve to pray for more workers because he knew the Father would listen to their prayers. He was welcoming them as partners of the kingdom.[18]

Still today God is calling and welcoming people into a partnership with him to effect change in this world. Partnering with God is an exciting process. In your efforts with God he will use you to bring about the results that he wants and the desires of your heart. Yet some people are afraid to take any action for fear that it takes away from God's power and ends up looking like a self-fulfilling prayer. Simply because you are involved in the process makes it no less a miracle when the results you desire are found. Rather your partnership with God reveals how you have allowed God to use your life to be an answer to your prayers.

- Nehemiah who prayed for the broken walls of Jerusalem to be rebuilt became the chief architect, builder, and motivator.

- The disciples who prayed for workers in the harvest became those harvest workers.

The channel for prayer to be answered often comes through your very own life. You are the hands and fingers, feet and toes that God uses. Someone has said "he who prays and prays, but acts not on what he knows, is like the man who plans and plans, but never sows." God will do all he can do, when you do all that you can do. There are three areas that you must look at as you partner with God.

Take Initiative

> *"I want you to learn this lesson: A little extra sleep, a little more slumber, a little folding of the hands to rest—and poverty will pounce on you like a bandit; scarcity will attack you like an armed robber."*
>
> *-Proverbs 6:9-11, NLT*

This verse above comes in the context of observing the ant and learning from its wisdom. It does not wait to gather food until winter comes, but rather the ant is industrious and takes initiative to gather food in the summer.

In the Old Testament we find Joseph was much like the ant—being proactive, industrious, and taking initiative in meeting the food demands for the nation of

Egypt. God had given a dream to the Pharaoh, but the interpretation of the dream belonged to Joseph—his key administrator in the kingdom. In the book of Genesis chapter 41 we read this story:

> [25]Then Joseph said to Pharaoh, "The dreams of
> Pharaoh are one; God has shown Pharaoh what
> He is about to do: [26]The seven good cows are
> seven years, and the seven good heads are seven
> years; the dreams are one. [27]And the seven thin
> and ugly cows which came up after them are
> seven years, and the seven empty heads blighted
> by the east wind are seven years of famine.
> [28]This is the thing which I have spoken to
> Pharaoh. God has shown Pharaoh what He is
> about to do. [29]Indeed seven years of great plenty
> will come throughout all the land of Egypt; [30]but
> after them seven years of famine will arise, and
> all the plenty will be forgotten in the land of
> Egypt; and the famine will deplete the land…
>
> [46]Joseph was thirty years old when he stood
> before Pharaoh king of Egypt. And Joseph went
> out from the presence of Pharaoh, and went
> throughout all the land of Egypt. [47]Now in the
> seven plentiful years the ground brought forth
> abundantly. [48]So he gathered up all the food of
> the seven years which were in the land of Egypt,
> and laid up the food in the cities; he laid up in
> every city the food of the fields which
> surrounded them. [49]Joseph gathered very much
> grain, as the sand of the sea, until he stopped
> counting, for it was without number…

> [53]Then the seven years of plenty which were in the land of Egypt ended, [54]and the seven years of famine began to come, as Joseph had said. The famine was in all lands, but in all the land of Egypt there was bread. [55]So when all the land of Egypt was famished, the people cried to Pharaoh for bread. Then Pharaoh said to all the Egyptians, "Go to Joseph; whatever he says to you, do." [56]The famine was over all the face of the earth, and Joseph opened all the storehouses and sold to the Egyptians. And the famine became severe in the land of Egypt. [57]So all countries came to Joseph in Egypt to buy grain, because the famine was severe in all lands. (NKJV)

In seeking out the needs of your life God challenges you to be like the ant, to be like Joseph who took initiative. Ask God to meet your needs, but then take initiative in the things you are able to do.

> In the church I pastor at New Life in Stonewall, Manitoba, we made a faith goal at our congregational ministry team to see 30 people take the step of baptism in their life in 2008. We presented this request to God in prayer, but then did not sit idly by and wait for people to respond. We made announcements to challenge people in this step of faith, created opportunities, and personally invited people. Although we did not quite reach 30, it was amazing because 26 people were baptized, which was a 100% increase from the year before!

When I reflect on the parable Jesus told about the man who needed bread for his travelling friend I see how he learned a valuable lesson on how to take initiative in meeting needs. Although we do not know exactly when this friend came to his house, it is possible that he came much earlier than midnight. At first this man's lack of action put him in a predicament, because he was without food. Most likely he could have bought food earlier, but his procrastination put him in a dilemma. Now, however, rather than sitting in the house and both of them looking at empty plates he took action. Although it was midnight he went to his neighbour's house to ask for bread.

Where in your life do you need to take greater initiative to finding solutions to your needs? Is it a roadblock at work, mending a relationship, overcoming an addiction, developing a hobby, or growing in God? Step out in faith and see what God will do. You will be surprised!

Give Your Best

"You must present as the LORD's portion the best and holiest part of everything given to you."
-Numbers 18:29, NIV

The context of this verse is a command given to the Levites—servants of God in the Temple. As the Israelites gave of their resources to support the Levites, the Levites in turn were to present the best of what they received to the Lord. God gave his best to them, and they were to give their best to God.

The apostle Paul, who considered himself the worst of sinners[19], experienced the immense mercy of God after his dramatic conversion on the Damascus road. In that moment he made the decision to give God the best of his life in times of plenty and in times of want, in times of ease and in times of difficulty. At the end of his life he writes in 2 Timothy 4:7-8 “I have fought the good fight, I have finished the race, I have kept the faith. Now there is in store for me the crown of righteousness, which the Lord, the righteous Judge, will award to me on that day.” God gave his best to Paul, and in return Paul gave his best to God.

There is an old hymn that speaks to the truth of giving God your best. In the hymn *Give of Your Best to the Master* written by Howard B. Grose he writes

1. *Give of your best to the Master;*
   Give of the strength of your youth;
   Throw your soul's fresh, glowing ardour
   Into the battle for truth.
   Jesus has set the example,
   Dauntless was He, young and brave;
   Give Him your loyal devotion;
   Give Him the best that you have.

2. *Give of your best to the Master;*
   Give Him first place in your heart;
   Give Him first place in your service;
   Consecrate every part.
   Give, and to you will be given;
   God His beloved Son gave;
   Gratefully seeking to serve Him,
   Give Him the best that you have.

3. *Give of your best to the Master;*
Naught else is worthy His love;
He gave Himself for your ransom,
Gave up His glory above.
Laid down His life without murmur,
You from sin's ruin to save;
Give Him your heart's adoration;
Give Him the best that you have.

Refrain:
Give of your best to the Master;
Give of the strength of your youth;
Clad in salvation's full armour,
Join in the battle for truth.

To experience God's blessings more fully you must be willing to give him your best. Do you short-change your efforts in working alongside God? Do you want things from God, but are unwilling to give back to him? Do your best so that God can bring about his best.

Giving God your best also means you are willing to offer God your resources, abilities, and expertise in finding solutions to the needs around you. God has all the power and resources to meet needs, but his resources are often given in the hands of his people. Often prayer is answered as God's people allow the things he has given them to be used in his service.

- The prayers for a new college might be answered through someone with organizational abilities.

- The prayers for building expansion might be answered through someone with the gift of generosity and ability to make large sums of money.

- The prayers for overcoming discouragement might be answered through someone who has the gift of encouragement.

God spreads out his gifts and resources to all believers. 1 Corinthians 12:7 says "A spiritual gift is given to each of us as a means of helping the entire church" (NLT). This way no one is overburdened in trying to meet every need. As God prompts your spirit to respond to a certain need or prayer, it is likely you are chosen, because God has given you that gift or resource to meet the need.

God's desire is that you become active with the things you have in finding the solutions to your prayers. The book of James says "faith without works is dead."[20] I think this might be true for prayer also. Prayer without works is dead.

What good is it to pray for someone in need and then do nothing about it? What good is it to pray for someone who is discouraged, but never do anything to encourage them? James 2:15-16 says, "Suppose a brother or sister is without clothes and daily food. If one of you says to him, 'Go, I wish you well; keep warm and well fed,' but does nothing about his physical needs, what good is it? In the same say, faith by itself, if it is not accompanied by action, is dead."

I was reminded of this principle a few years ago when I prayed for a job for a university student in Saskatoon. He was a foreign student who hoped to find a job in Canada. As I prayed for a job for him God challenged me to go beyond prayer and become active in helping him find one.

And so beyond prayer I became active. I took him down to the employment centre and to the *Open Door Society,* an organization that dealt specifically with foreigners looking for jobs. We received some good advice, and some possible leads for a job. The lady we talked with mentioned that their organization was built around networking. The more we could network, the better our chances of him finding a job, because it is not always in what you know, but in who you know.

His part in the process was to hand in an updated resume. Although no job came about through this organization, he did find a job when he was asked to be a sessional lecturer at the University of Saskatchewan, something far beyond what he or I even imagined. God was good!

Partnering with God means to put out your best in the process of prayer. In your action oriented prayer God may reward you far beyond what you thought possible. Ephesians 3:20 says “to him [God] who is able to do immeasurably more than all we ask or imagine, according to his power that is at work within us.”

Network with Others

"By helping each other with your troubles, you truly obey the law of Christ."

-Galatians 6:2, NCV

Sometimes it is not always in what you know, but in who you know. Prayer is often answered through a multitude of people involved in the process. No one has complete knowledge, resources, and ability to achieve what they need. Only God does. Anyone who has got somewhere has got there because someone else was involved. Unfortunately our society stresses independence, but God calls us to interdependence. You and I are to work alongside God and others to compliment each another with our gifts and help each other in times of need.

When you partner with someone else you will accomplish the task much quicker or find the answer much faster. The Bible says "two are better than one, because they have a good return for their work."[21] Your prayers will be answered more quickly as you learn to network with others.

This principle reminds me of one of the games played at a Junior Camp I used to direct. Basically it is a spin-off from hide-and-seek. All the counsellors hide throughout the campground and all the children try to find them and bring them back for points. The more kids that are out searching together the better their chances at finding their counsellor.

It is the same principle used in finding missing persons or scattered debris from plane wreckages. Volunteers line up at arm's length and then walk together scanning over their path for any clues. One person walking alone makes the search almost futile, but with many people the search becomes promising.

> A few months ago I was in quite the dilemma. It all started out good. It was a beautiful day in February with the snow melting to slush. Before going back to work I did some errands downtown. As I got back to my office in the church I took off my winter gloves only to discover that my wedding ring was no longer with me. I didn't like the thought of telling my wife this news, as it was right before Valentine's Day!
>
> I checked the parking lot and foyer of the church, but to no avail. In my mind I retraced my steps and figured it must have come off in one of two places—either at the town office or post office where I had taken off my gloves. I mentioned to some of the office staff to pray that I might find it and then I went back to look for it.
>
> As I was walking and praying I was expectant that God would reveal it to me. I thought of my Dad who lost his wedding ring, only to find it 10 years later while rototilling the garden. I was hoping mine might show up sooner! Well I went to the town office, but nothing was found there. The receptionist did promise to tell the janitor to keep an eye out for it.

Next I went to the Post Office to look, but again nothing showed up. I mentioned to friends at a local business to keep their eyes posted for it. I thought it may have fallen off in the slush somewhere outside their store in the parking lot. Things were not looking promising.

As I went back to the car I prayed one last prayer to God. I said, "God I am not able to find this ring and it seems impossible that I will, so could you use someone else to find it for me in a place that I have not looked." I then picked up enough courage and phoned my wife to tell her the not-so-good news.

The next day I returned to the office and about a half hour later our director of facilities comes into my office asking if I knew of anyone who had lost a wedding ring. I almost fell off my chair! "I did!" I exclaimed. "Amen! Praise the Lord!" I shouted out. It was a great day and a great answer to prayer. I then asked him where he found it. He mentioned it was underneath the book table on which copies of my first book *Lifestyle of Prayer* were laying.

How it got there I don't know, other than it must have fallen into my clothing or onto my boot, and then finally slipped off as I entered the foyer of our church. Either that or God sent his angel to put it in a place where he would use someone to find it in a place that I had not looked.

In your prayers God can and will use others to become the answers to your requests. Keep your eyes open to not only how God is meeting your needs, but whom he might be using as well.

What are the needs you see in your life and this world? Can you meet them more quickly or better by partnering with someone else? Take time to write out a list of your needs and desires. Then in a column next to this write down whom you can partner with to reach these objectives.

GOING DEEPER

"Seek in Partnership"

1. In what ways can inaction result in unanswered prayer?

2. What things hold you back from taking initiative in becoming the answer to your prayers?

3. List one or two areas in your life where you need to step out in faith and work at meeting the needs in your life or that of someone else.

4. In what ways can a person fail to give God their best and miss out on the blessings of God?

5. Tell of a time where God answered your prayer above what you imagined or expected.

6. Tell of a time when God used someone else to answer a prayer of yours.

7. Write out your prayer requests in one column and then in the next column list people you can network with to meet this request.

DETERMINE YOUR DIRECTION THROUGH KNOCKING

In Carolyn Arends song, *Seize the Day*, she writes:

I know a girl who was schooled in Manhattan
She reads dusty books and learns phrases in Latin
She is an author or maybe a poet
A genius but its just this world doesn't know it
She works on her novel most every day
If you laugh she will say

> *Seize the day*
> *Seize whatever you can*
> *Cause life slips away just like hourglass sand*
> *Seize the day pray for grace from God's hand*
> *That nothin' will stand in your way*
> *Seize the day*

Well I know a doctor a fine young physician
Left his six figure job for a mission position
He's healin' the sick in an African clinic
He works in the dirt and writes home to the cynics
He says we work through the night almost every day
As we watch the sun rise we can say

> *Seize the day*
> *Seize whatever you can*
> *Cause life slips away just like hourglass sand*
> *Seize the day pray for grace from God's hand*
> *That nothin' will stand in your way*
> *Seize the day*

Well I know a man who's been doin' some thinkin'
He's as bitter and cold as the whisky he's drinkin'
He's talkin' bout fear 'bout chances not taken
If you listen to him you can hear his heart breakin'

He says "One day you're a boy the next day you're dead
I wish way back when someone had said..."

Seize the day
Seize whatever you can
Cause life slips away just like hourglass sand
Seize the day pray for grace from God's hand
That nothin' will stand in your way
Seize the day

Well one thing I've noticed wherever I wander
Everyone's got a dream he can follow or squander
You can do what you will with the days you are given
I'm tryin' to spend mine on the business of livin'
So I'm singin' my songs off of any old stage
You can laugh if you want He'll still say

Seize the day
Seize whatever you can
Cause life slips away just like hourglass sand
Seize the day pray for grace from God's hand
That nothin' will stand in your way
Seize the day[22]

Prayer is to seize the opportunities that God places before you and to work alongside God in meeting needs. In this third step in the strategy of prayer you must courageously knock to determine God's direction. God has planned opportunities for you to make a difference, receive a blessing, or meet a need. It is in these moments of opportunity that God calls you to seize the day. Don't let life slip you by. Knock and God will open the door to many wonderful things.

Knock with Confidence

"Let us then approach the throne of grace with confidence, so that we may receive mercy and find grace to help us in our time of need."

-Hebrews 4:16, NIV

As I reflect on the parable of the man who went to his neighbour's house at midnight, I find that his needs were met because he had the courage to knock. This man would have been foolish to go to his neighbour's house and never rap his knuckles on the door. He had to at least try and see if this was the place where his needs would be met. He knocked, the door was opened, and the bread was given.

At times you may feel you have found the solution to your requests. Yet you will never know until you determine to check it out. Perhaps this is the moment in which God will meet your desires. You need to test the waters. You need to knock and if the door opens then you have received God's blessing, but if it does not open at this spot then try another.

What is it that keeps you from moving forward in God's direction and blessing for your life? Too often people feel they have found the solution to their needs only to walk away empty handed. In the next few pages I want to address three attitudes that you need to overcome in order to realize the answers to your requests.

Overcome an Attitude of Failure

"Then Peter got down out of the boat, walked on the water and came toward Jesus."
-Matthew 14:29, NIV

It's easy to hold back and not look the fool, but greater blessings are given to those who try risking failure. One of the attitudes that this man in Jesus' parable had to overcome was the fear of failure. How would he look if he came back to his travelling guest empty-handed without any bread? Was it even possible to get three loaves of bread from his friend at midnight? Would his friend be awake to hear his knock and if he heard his knock would he have enough bread? Yet his need for bread was greater than all the doubts and fears he had. All he could do was give it a try and see what happened.

Self-image plays a big part in a person's ability to knock. No one wants to be rejected. No one wants to fail. No one wants to be embarrassed. Yet a person must overcome these fears so that they can open God's blessings for their lives. If the only areas a person moved forward in were things that guaranteed 100% success, most people would miss out on 99% of what God has in store for them.

Life is full of uncertainties except God and his faithfulness to you. God wants you to work alongside him in meeting your desires and the needs of others. Yes you might fail in plans outside his will, but God will not fail you in plans inside his will. In building the temple, David encouraged his son Solomon with these words found in 1 Chronicles 29:20:

> "Be strong and courageous, and do the work. Do not be afraid or discouraged, for the LORD God, my God, is with you. He will not fail you or forsake you until all the work for the service of the temple of the LORD is finished." (NIV)

God will continue to stay with you until you find his best. He promises to never fail you or forsake you. Peter moved past his doubts, focused on Jesus, and walked on water. Solomon overcame his fears, trusted in God, and built the temple. You can do the same.

At times you do not know what the response will be in regards to your requests. You may have asked God and have found the solution, but now comes the moment of decision. Are you ready to be embarrassed, rejected, and fail when you knock? Too many times people have found that ideal job, life-long mate, or perfect solution, but fail to realize it because they were afraid to pursue it. Another job passes them by, because they do not want to fail in the interview. Another potential mate slips away, because they fear rejection. Another great opportunity fades away because they do not want to be embarrassed in trying. You must look failure straight in the face and step out in courage to reach your goals.

> Ted Williams, one of baseball's all-time best hitters, failed six times out of ten in his best year when he batted .400!

In the 1940's, two brothers named Dick and Maurice MacDonald were ready to call it quits in the restaurant business. They kept going and hired a third partner, Ray Kroc, who had creative ideas. Today the "Golden Arches" with their hamburgers can be found world-wide.

Glenn Cunningham was burned so severely in a school fire that doctors said he would never walk again. Yet in 1934 he set a world record by running a mile in 4 minutes, 6.8 seconds.

Albert Einstein was called a slow learner, and even retarded. Yet he went on to become one of the world's greatest scientists that ever lived. His theory of relativity has revolutionized the world of physics.

Beethoven's music teacher said "As a composer he's hopeless." Today he is one of the best loved composers of classical music.

Thomas Edison did not do well in school, but today he is known as one of the greatest inventors of modern technology. Through his genius he developed the electric light bulb, electric generating system, phonograph, and motion picture projector.

In their book, *You Don't Have to Quit*, Anne and Ray Ortlund give some helpful tips on how to reach your desires even when it looks impossible.

1. *Begin with prayer.* Seek God's mind from the start.
2. *Define as specifically as you can what you're about to do.* If there are steps in the process, rank them in order of importance.
3. *Tell several people close to you what you hope to do.* You need the accountability and prayer support of a special few.
4. *Begin some little part of your project immediately.* Even a small step is a step. And if possible, do something toward your project every single work day, to keep it always before you.
5. *Give yourself deadlines, and let your supporters know your deadlines.* Both the prayer and the pressure will be great motivators! But if you miss a deadline or fail at a part of your project along the way, don't be too discouraged.
6. *Anticipate all the troubles you can.* Be calmly realistic to know they're coming.

> *A sensible man watches for problems ahead and prepares to meet them. The simpleton never looks, and suffers the consequences* (Prov. 27:12 TLB).[23]

Overcome an Attitude of Disability

"I can do all things through Christ who strengthens me."

-Philippians 4:13, NKJV

I am amazed at some of the incredible feats that people with disabilities have accomplished. I enjoyed watching the 2010 Winter Olympics that were held in Vancouver, Canada and the things that that these athletes accomplished. I was equally amazed at the paralympians who competed two weeks later. Their agility, despite missing limbs, was impressive to watch.

One Canadian downhill skier, Lauren Woolstencroft, has captured the hearts of not only Canadians, but people throughout the world. Born without legs below the knees and one arm below her elbow she demonstrated her speed and ability on the ski slopes. She once said that "if you can hear the crowd then you're going way too slow." Her skiing philosophy worked as she captured a record five paralympic gold medals, permanently giving her the nickname the "Golden Girl." I am amazed at these athletes. They can do better with their disability than I can with my ability!

Another man in my home province of Manitoba has also done a remarkable feat in the political sphere. On October 4, 2004 Steven Fletcher made the history books of Canada as he became the first quadriplegic ever to be elected to Canada's parliament. Although completely disabled from the neck down after a horrific car accident involving a giant moose crossing the highway, he went on to campaign with the Conservative government and was elected to Canada's parliament.

Everyone has a disability in some form. What are your physical or emotional limitations? What might be impossible to you is not impossible with God. Jesus said in Matthew 19:26 "with man this is impossible, but with God all things are possible." Do not let your disabilities keep you from moving forward in God's plan for your life. God can give you the strength to work past these barriers and accomplish his purpose for your life.

John Eldridge put out a little book called *You Have What It Takes*. In a couple sections he writes

> Look at the stories boys love, the games they play. They are full of battle and adventure and danger. They love to build things…and then blow 'em up. They love to jump off stuff. What does a boy wear if you let him wear what he *wants* to wear? Let him out of his school clothes and his Sunday school togs, and in a moment he'll be decked out in camouflage, army style, or dressed up as a cowboy, a fireman, a superhero, a Jedi knight with a bath towel wrapped around him and a stern look in his eye. Every boy wants to be a hero. Every boy wants to be powerful, he wants to be dangerous, he wants to know: *Do I have what it takes?*
>
> …You see, no matter how old you are, no matter how much you have (or have not) achieved, *you* still have a Question. Do *you* have what it takes? The only one who can really settle that for you is God. You must ask God. And you must stay with The Question until you get an answer.[24]

Knocking with confidence means you must move past your fears of capability to experience God's blessings. You might have to wrestle with questions like 'Can I handle this? Do I have what it takes? Am I smart enough?' and on may go the list of these self-doubting questions. Some people fear job promotions and transitions wondering if they will be able to fulfill the job requirements. Other people fear getting married and having children wondering if they can handle the daily responsibilities. God will never give you more than you can handle, but you will never know what you can handle if you are unwilling to try. God knows your potential even when you do not.

Moses did not think he could ever lead the Israelite people out of Egypt, yet he did and became one of Israel's greatest leaders. God helped Moses overcome an attitude of disability by addressing three self-image problems he wallowed in.

- *Lack of Influence* - Moses underestimated his ability to influence the Egyptian Pharaoh in letting the Israelite people go. Moses said to God in Exodus 3:11, "*Who am I, that I should go to Pharaoh* and bring the Israelites out of Egypt." God responds in the next verse "I will be with you." The ability to influence others for God is not in and of ourselves, but in the power of God working through us.

- *Lack of Authority* - Moses feared the Israelite people would not listen to his message because he was not viewed as a credible leader. In Exodus 4:1 Moses responds to God *"What if they do not believe me or listen to me* and say, 'The Lord did not appear to you?'" To silence his doubts God confirmed Moses' leadership authority through three miraculous wonders—turning his staff into a snake, making his hand become leprous, and turning water into blood. God said in Exodus 4:8-9, "If they do not believe you or pay attention to the first miraculous sign, they may believe the second. But if they do not believe these two signs or listen to you, take some water from the Nile and pour it on the dry ground. The water you take from the river will become blood on the ground." God was building skills into Moses life that would give him the necessary authority to fulfill his responsibility. God will also build skills into your life to accomplish the tasks that are before you.

- *Lack of Communication* – A third area of self-doubt that Moses faced was his ability to communicate. Moses feared that he could not give direction to this large group of people because he lacked communication skills. In Exodus 4:10 Moses says to God, *"O Lord, I have never been eloquent,* neither in the past nor since you have spoken to your servant. I am slow of speech and tongue." This last response angered God because Moses was using every excuse to avoid becoming God's instrument to free the Israelites. Yet God was willing to train Moses further. In Exodus 4:15 God says "You shall speak to him [Aaron] and put words in his mouth; I will help both of you

> speak and will teach you what to do." In time Moses mastered this skill of communication and went before hundreds of thousands of people to deliver God's message. When you think you can't do it God will bring others alongside you to help you in your task.

I find that God usually takes me step by step in fulfilling the plans he has for my life. Each time as I respond to that inner tug to try something God provides me strength, develops my skills, and encourages me through others that I have what it takes to handle this new level of responsibility. God prepares you and me for increasingly greater work but it can only happen through our willingness to knock and give it a try.

Overcome an Attitude of Despair

> *"Consider it pure joy, my brothers, whenever you face trials of many kinds, because you know that the testing of your faith develops perseverance. Perseverance must finish its work so that you may be mature and complete, not lacking anything."*
>
> *-James 1:2-4, NIV*

A young woman made an appointment for an interview with a prestigious corporation. She asked if she could get into their well-respected training program. The very busy personnel manager, besieged by applications, said, "Impossible now. Come back in about ten years." The applicant responded, "Would morning or afternoon be better?"[25]

Another attitude which can keep you from experiencing God's blessings is trials that produce despair and immobilize you to carry on. It is in times like this that you need perseverance to overcome negative thinking and despairing situations. The reward of perseverance is maturity, completeness, not lacking anything as the book of James states.

Most times the things you ask God for are right, but it is not the right timing. And so don't give up after one attempt, but keep knocking. Maybe in ten years, five years, or only one year the timing will be right and God will grant you your request. Years ago a…

> …mission serving in the southern Sudan was expelled by the government, but its workers did not cease praying that the door might reopen. Ten years later they were invited back by the very same government that ousted them![26]

A closed door does not always mean it is the end of the matter. So keep on knocking. It took perseverance for this man to receive the blessing of bread from his friend. The man could have given up and gone home after the owner said the doors are locked and my children are in bed. Yet because of the man's persistence the neighbour got out of bed and gave him what was needed. In the end he lacked nothing.

In my former church in Saskatoon I received a small wallet sized card from a member entitled "Don't Quit." It has reminded me to keep going and knocking at the doors of opportunity before me when things tend to look futile through the eyes of discouragement.

When things go wrong as they sometimes will.
When the road you're trudging seems all uphill.
When the funds are low and the debts are high,
And you want to smile, but you have to sigh.
When care is pressing you down a bit—
Rest if you must, but don't you quit.

Success is failure turned inside out,
The silver tint of the clouds of doubt,
And you never can tell how close you are
It may be near when it seems afar.
So stick to the fight when you're hardest hit—
It's when things go wrong that you mustn't quit.

GOING DEEPER

"Knock with Confidence"

1. What attitude do you need to overcome in stepping out in action to become the solution to your requests—fear of failure, disability, or despair?

2. In what ways can a poor self-image hinder your prayer life and keep you from experiencing God's blessings?

3. Tell of a time when you overcame the fear of failing and stepped out with courage to do something.

4. Who is someone with a disability that you admire for their confidence? What lessons do you learn from their life?

5. List the areas in your life where you doubt your ability to make it through. Ask God to give you strength.

6. Tell of a prayer request of yours that was answered months or years later.

7. What prayer requests do you have right now that you need hope to keep pressing forward?

KNOCK WITH MOTIVATION

"Brothers, I do not consider myself yet to have taken hold of it. But one thing I do: Forgetting what is behind and straining toward what is ahead, I press on toward the goal to win the prize for which God has called me heavenward in Christ Jesus."

-Philippians 3:13-14, NIV

Many things are accomplished in life through the art of motivation. Rewards are incentives for people to try something new or to keep going along the pathway of their dreams. Kids often clean up their rooms or do other things for their parents because a weekly allowance or trip to the ice cream store awaits them. Students write many papers and read numerous books in university because they envision working in a certain career. NHL players endure gruelling games, sore bodies, and give it all they've got so they have the chance to hoist the Stanley Cup over their head. Astronauts will train for years waiting for that special moment to be called to become part of a flight crew into space and the chance to see earth from afar.

It was the dream of a better day that motivated a black Baptist pastor and peace activist, Martin Luther King Jr., to give one of the most notable and memorable speeches in American history called "I Have a Dream." In this speech on August 28, 1963 he envisions a future where blacks, whites, and other groups of people would coexist harmoniously as equals. In this speech he alludes to various scriptures proclaiming freedom and justice.

- It came as a joyous daybreak to end the long night of their captivity (Psalm 30:5)

- We will not be satisfied until justice rolls down like waters and righteousness like a mighty stream. (Amos 5:24)

- I have a dream that every valley shall be exalted. (Isaiah 40:4).

Some of his other key phrases in this now famous speech are:

> *"When the architects of our republic wrote the magnificent words of the Constitution and the Declaration of Independence, they were signing a promissory note to which every American was to fall heir. This note was a promise that all men—yes, black men as well as white men—would be guaranteed the unalienable rights of life, liberty and the pursuit of happiness."*

> *"I have a dream that one day this nation will rise up and live out the true meaning of its creed: 'We hold these truths to be self-evident, that all men are created equal.'"*

> *"I have a dream that my four little children will one day live in a nation where they will not be judged by the color of their skin, but by the content of their character."*

> *"Now is the time to lift our nation from the quicksand of racial injustice to the solid rock of*

brotherhood. Now is the time to make justice a reality for all of God's children."

"Let freedom ring. And when this happens, and when we allow freedom ring—when we let it ring from every village and every hamlet, from every state and every city, we will be able to speed up that day when all of God's children—black men and white men, Jews and Gentiles, Protestants and Catholics—will be able to join hands and sing in the words of the old Negro spiritual: 'Free at last! Free at last! Thank God Almighty, we are free at last!'"[27]

Although Martin Luther King Jr. was assassinated on April 4, 1968 for his beliefs, others carried on his dream for equality and the civil rights movement. Just over 45 years later his dream reached reality when Barak Obama was inaugurated on January 20, 2009 as the first ever African-American president of the United States. In only one generation it is amazing what can happen when someone steps out and pursues a dream of their heart.

Most people will train harder, give more, and wait longer when they perceive the benefits in doing so. The Apostle Paul suffered much at the hands of others for his faith in Christ, but he kept going for the prize that awaited him one day in heaven. Jesus endured his painful death on the cross, because he was motivated in destroying Satan's works and offering salvation to everyone in every generation.

If you can anticipate the benefits in your prayers being answered then it should give you the courage to try. I believe there are two reasons that will motivate you to work alongside God and test your opportunities.

Knocking Reveals God's Will

> *"Do not conform any longer to the pattern of this world, but be transformed by the renewing of your mind. Then you will be able to test and approve what God's will is—his good, pleasing and perfect will."*
>
> *-Romans 12:2, NIV*

In knocking you determine God's direction in your life. I love this verse in 1 John 5:14-15 and how action-oriented prayer is related to discovering God's will. It says "This is the confidence we have in approaching God: that if we ask anything according to his will, he hears us. And if we know that he hears us—whatever we ask—we know that we have what we asked of him." Prayer is about helping you move into the centre of God's will for your life. If you fail to knock you will fail to know God's direction for your life.

When I face major decisions in my life I ask God to either open or close the door so that I might know his will for my life. As I look back on my life there have been employers who turned me down, girls who have said no to a date, and opportunities that I could not take. The doors closed and at the moment it happened I was not sure why. Yet in hindsight I understand God's plan. Today I am filled with joy for I am in a career that I greatly enjoy, have a wife and family that I dearly love, and countless opportunities that expand my horizon. I would never have known God's will for my life until I risked stepping out to knock on the door.

Yet you need to be careful that you do not pry open doors that are not intended for you. You can become so driven that you end up in a place or with a person that is not meant for you. Do not force a door open because it may not be where God wants you. This might not be the place where your needs are best met.

There often is a fine line between being persistent in prayer and being foolishly aggressive. How do you know when to back away from a prayer that is not being answered immediately?

First if your heart is not at peace and you do not feel right about what you want or are asking then it is time stop. Listen to your conscience. Are you at peace with this prayer? Can you honestly continue to persist? 1 John 4:21-22 says "Dear friends, if our hearts do not condemn us, we have confidence before God and receive from him anything we ask, because we obey his commands and do what pleases him."

Secondly it is time to stop when you recognize that by not having this prayer answered God is teaching you life lessons and developing your character. Are you able to accept your situation? Part of God's will may involve temporary suffering in this world. The apostle Paul knew when to back off from praying so that God could more powerfully work through his life. In 2 Corinthians 12:7-9 Paul writes

> To keep me from becoming conceited because of these surpassingly great revelations, there was given me a thorn in my flesh, a messenger of Satan, to torment me. Three times I pleaded with the Lord to take it away from me. But he said to me, “My grace is sufficient for you, for my power is made perfect in weakness.”

Joni Tada Eareckson became a quadriplegic after diving into a shallow, rock filled bay. For months she struggled with her condition, and cried out desperately for God to heal her. Yet the door of healing did not happen. In time as her heart was healed toward God, she came to accept her physical condition. Today Joni is still a quadriplegic, but as she reflects on her experience, she says it is one of the best things that could have happened to her. In her autobiography she writes “I wouldn't change my life for anything. I even feel privileged...I'm really thankful He did something to get my attention and change me.”[28] Through this experience she came so much closer to God and is now used by him to speak all over the world telling about the grace of God.

Third it is time to stop praying when the burden of your prayer is lifted. God may have you pray for something or someone for years, because each day that burden is on your soul. Yet there may come a point when you no longer have the same sense of urgency to pray for a certain request. Either God has lightened your load by placing that burden on someone else to pray for, or what was asked has been fulfilled, is no longer needed, or is not an issue.

You might think you know what you want, but God knows what you need. At times the doors you want opened will not open. You need to be content in that and continue to knock in other places to find God's will. You might think this is the job for me and it falls through. Well God may have a bigger and better purpose for your life. You may think this is the man or woman I will marry. It may not work out because God has someone who will better meet your needs and who will be compatible with you. You may want more money, a bigger house, many children, and a host of other things. Sometimes these doors open and sometimes they do not, because God sees the bigger picture of your life. He knows what will help you, and he knows what will destroy you.

Yet even in the wrong doors of choice God can lead you back to the right doors where you will find his purpose. Do not despair, but give your all to finding God's will for your life today. He can heal the hurts of past mistakes, wrong choices, or other tragedies and give you grace to experience a greater day ahead.

Knocking Unleashes God's Blessings

"Every good and perfect gift is from above, coming down from the Father of the heavenly lights, who does not change like shifting shadows."

-James 1:17, NIV

Knocking not only helps you find God's place for your life, but it also unleashes God's blessing to you. Untold good things await you on the other side of prayer. In this third step of prayer you will need to move out in courage to open God's resources and believe that what you receive will be his best.

In Matthew 7:7-11 Jesus uses an illustration to underscore the fact that God our Father cares for us and will not give something that will harm us. Jesus says

> 7Ask and it will be given to you; seek and you will find; knock and the door will be opened to you. 8For everyone who asks receives; he who seeks finds; and to him who knocks, the door will be opened.
>
> 9Which of you, if his son asks for bread, will give him a stone? 10Or if he asks for a fish, will give him a snake? 11If you, then, though you are evil, know how to give good gifts to your children, how much more will your Father in heaven give good gifts to those who ask him!

Jesus uses this humorous illustration to point out the fact that even an earthly father knows how to give good gifts to his children. If a son asks his dad for some bread because he is hungry, will his father give him a stone? A round stone might resemble a loaf of bread, but sink your teeth into it and you will have none left! Would a father be that cruel? Or if a hungering son were to ask for some fish, would his dad hand him a snake, which might be the eel-like catfish of Galilee that was considered unclean to eat? Would a father mock his son like that? Jesus says even though earthly fathers are sinful by nature, they still know how to give good gifts to their sons and daughters. As fathers we give because we love our children. They are our own. Billy Graham writes

> There were children in our neighbourhood for whom I provided all clothing, food, and the necessities of life. They asked freely of me and their requests were usually granted. They were my children! By virtue of their relationship to me, I had a particular responsibility to them.[29]

When you receive Jesus into your life and live to follow him, you are born into God's family and become his children. In the gospel of John 1:12-13 it says “yet to all who received him, to those who believed in his name, he gave the right to become children of God—children born not of natural descent, nor of human decision or a husband's will, but born of God.” Because you are God’s child he will take good care of you.

In this illustration above Jesus makes the comparison between an earthly father and our heavenly Father. If earthly fathers who are sinful by nature know how to give what is good to their children then how much more will our heavenly Father, who has no sin, give what is good to us!

One of the hardest things some people face is getting past an unhealthy view of what God is like. Many people believe God will answer their prayer requests in a vindictive and cruel way. He will give them a stone when they ask for bread or a snake when they ask for fish. Since they have failed or sinned in some way they believe God is out to get them. Millard J. Erickson in his classic work of *Christian Theology* writes, "some people think of God as a kind of celestial policeman who looks for opportunities to pounce upon erring and straying persons."[30]

Yet did we not, as children, hurt our parents and still they provided for our needs? Why do we think at times that God who is perfect and sinless is so vindictive? What makes us think that God will mock or refuse to bless us by meeting our needs? Is not Satan trying to blind our eyes?

If this is an area in which you struggle about God's nature ask him to change your perception of who he is. God is not a vindictive, out-to-get-you God, but a heavenly Father who has unconditional love for his children. You can be confident that God will reveal that answer, provide that solution, and open that door, because he loves you. It is in God's willingness to respond with good things that should give you the motivation to knock.

GOING DEEPER

"Knock with Motivation"

1. What dreams or goals do you have for your life? What motivates you to achieve these dreams?

2. How do you know when to back away or keep going in a prayer that is not being answered immediately?

3. How does knocking in prayer reveals God's will for your life?

4. Tell of a time when you forced open a door only to realize this was not God's will. In what ways did God try and get your attention about your choice?

5. What reasons is God motivated to bless you with good things?

6. What are some gifts your parents gave to you? How did this reveal their love for you?

7. How does Satan try and blind you to the good nature of God?

KNOCK WITH DISCERNMENT

"Cast all your anxiety on him because he cares for you."

-1 Peter 5:7, NIV

There are many things that I let my kids play with, but there are some things I do not give them because they do not understand how it can hurt them. My oldest daughter when she was about two years old liked to play with empty pop cans. I let her until the day she figured out how to break the metal tabs off and put them in her mouth. I still let her play with the pop cans, but only after the tabs had been taken off. I did not give her the whole can until she matured more and was responsible enough to use it wisely. I did not take away the pop cans because I was mean, but because I cared enough to protect her from serious injury.

Sometimes you will receive what you want right away from the hand of God, but at other times it may seem as if nothing happens. When a prayer is not answered as you think it should you may feel God does not care about you. God is not, however, like that. As a Father he will give what is best for your life and protect you from things that will harm or keep you from growing spiritually. Bill Hybels gives a good synopsis on how to discern the response of God to your prayers.

> If the request is wrong, God says, "No."
> If the timing is wrong, God says, "Slow."
> If you are wrong, God says, "Grow."
> But if the request is right, the timing is right and you are right, God says, "Go!"[31]

God's response to your prayers can be viewed in one of three ways—no, wait, or yes. You will need to adjust your life to each response so that you stay within the will of God.

No Means Never

> *"When you spread out your hands in prayer, I will hide my eyes from you; even if you offer many prayers, I will not listen. Your hands are full of blood; wash and make yourselves clean. Take your evil deeds out of my sight! Stop doing wrong."*
>
> *-Isaiah 1:15-16, NIV*

It is difficult at times to tell if a request that is not answered is a flat out "no" which means "never," or if it is a conditional "no" that means "wait." When a request of yours is not being answered as you think it should you will need to ask questions to discern God's response.

Is this request morally wrong for me or someone else?

Is this request outside the parameters of God's word?

Is this request going to lead me away from a vibrant relationship with God?

Is this request going to weaken my character and spiritual growth as a person?

God wants to give you what is best, but at times he must withhold things because he knows that what you want will keep you from growing spiritually. In the following poem it highlights the various reasons as to why God may say no to what you want.

I asked God to take away my habit.

God said, "No. It is not for me to take away, but for you to give it up"

I asked God to make my handicapped child whole.

God said, "No. His spirit is whole, his body is only temporary."

I asked God to grant me patience.

God said, "No. Patience is a byproduct of tribulations. It isn't granted, it is learned."

I asked God to give me happiness.

God said, "No. I give you blessings. Happiness is up to you."

I asked God to spare me pain.

God said, "No. Suffering draws you apart from worldly cares and brings you closer to me."

I asked God for all things that I might enjoy life.

God said, "No. I will give you life, so that you may enjoy all things."

I asked God to help me LOVE others, as much as He loves me.

God said..."Ahhhh, finally you have the idea."

Wait Means Later

"I wait for you, O LORD; you will answer, O Lord my God."

-Psalm 38:15, NIV

If the timing is wrong, or the motives tainted, then God may give you a "no" with a conditional "slow" and "grow" attached. There are a few reasons why God may withhold a favourable answer to your prayer requests.

One reason that your prayers may go unanswered is that God wants you to grow in your love for him. If all you want is the gift and not the Giver, God may keep certain things from you. Jesus said in John 15:7 "If you remain in me and my words remain in you, ask whatever you wish, and it will be given you." Sometimes prayers are answered in your life once your desire to lovingly obey God overtakes your desire for other things. Jesus said in John 15:9-10a "As the Father has loved me, so have I loved you. Now remain in my love. If you obey my commands, you will remain in my love."

A second reason might be so that you grow in humility. You might not receive anything because your price is too high. You may want more than what God is willing to give. Is not something better than nothing? Greed often impairs judgment in prayer. Motives that are tainted with greed result in failed responses. James 4:3 says “When you ask, you do not receive, because you ask with wrong motives, that you may spend what you get on your pleasures.” God may want you to live on less, so that others with less may live on more.

A third reason you may have to wait in receiving things from God is that God wants you to grow in patience and dependence on him. Answers to prayer often include time adjustments. You want it now, but God may want you to learn how to trust and depend on him. Sometimes you may have to wait so that your life will mature to the point where you are ready to handle the gift with responsibility. My parents did not give me the keys to the car at the age of five, but waited until I was old enough, had taken my driver's education, and passed the driving exam.

A fourth reason an answer to prayer may not be forthcoming in your life is that God wants you to grow in your delight of him more than anything else. God’s desire is that you enjoy the Giver of gifts more than the gift itself. Psalm 37:4 says “Delight yourself in the Lord and he will give you the desires of your heart.” Are you enjoying your relationship with God? Do you love to work for Him? Do you find pleasure in reading His word? I know as a father, I more readily give things to my children when they enjoy my company.

Yes Means Now

> *"I have placed before you an open door that no one can shut. I know that you have little strength, yet you have kept my word and have not denied my name."*
>
> *-Revelation 3:8, NIV*

It is said of George Muller the man of faith and prayer…

> In countless cases, while he was on his knees asking, the answer has come in such close correspondence with the request as to shut out *chance* as an explanation, and compel belief in a prayer-hearing God…George Muller believed, and because he believed, prayed; and praying, expected; and expecting, received.[32]

The third response of God to your prayers is a resounding yes! God has many more things to give you than he has to keep from you. When you ask according to God's will, with pure motives and a mature attitude, God blesses you with a yes response. In this response the door opens and you walk into the will of God more deeply.

Every gift that you receive must be credited back to God for without him there would be no blessing, no open door. In Revelation 3:7b-8 it says

> These are the words of him who is holy and true, who holds the key of David. What he opens no one can shut, and what he shuts no one can open.

> I know your deeds. See, I have placed before you an open door that no one can shut. I know that you have little strength, yet you have kept my word and have not denied my name.

These verses portray the type of life you must live to hear the "yes" of God.

Obedience to God's Word: "You have kept my word." God opens the door and gives his reward when you have a strong desire to follow all his ways. In times of weakness it is to keep obeying the Word despite the ridicule, doubt, or hardship you face.

Faithfulness to God's Name: "[You] have not denied my name." God opens the door and gives his reward when you remain faithful to him. In times of weakness it is to identify with God even when it may cost you—increased hardship, loss of friends, or missed opportunities.

GOING DEEPER

"Knock with Discernment"

1. How does God's response to your prayers guide you in praying?

2. Tell of a time when God said no to a request of yours and you understand the reasons for it now.

3. What are some reasons that God will say no to a request of yours?

4. What are the four reasons why God may not answer a prayer of yours immediately?

5. What prayer of yours is not answered yet and which of the four reasons listed above might God want you to grow in before it is answered?

6. List the prayer requests that God has said yes to you. Take time to thank him for these.

7. What two things can you do to see God respond more favourably to your requests?

CONCLUSION

Prayer starts with God (ask), continues with God (seek), and ends with God (knock). Never give up on finding God's blessings for your life.

Years ago when I finished my Masters degree from Prairie Bible Institute in Calgary, Alberta I hoped to find a church to serve in as a pastor. I handed my resume to one denomination's head office who would forward it to churches looking for pastors. I left it at that and just waited to hear something. I waited and waited and waited. Finally I contacted the head office to find out what was taking so long. I realized that somewhere along the line it was misunderstood that I was seeking only an associate position, rather than being open to a senior pastor position as well. By the time this was cleared up, I wasted valuable months, missed a great number of opportunities, and ended up with the last church available, one that proved to be very difficult. After just over a year in this church I knew it was time to resign, take a leap of faith into the unknown, and see what God had in store for me.

My wife and I moved to Regina, Saskatchewan and for the next 10 months I was in limbo, without a permanent position. In the meantime God provided me a job through a friend's father who owned a carpet company. I was glad for this job, for it provided necessary income for both my wife and I. Yet I still had a burning desire to be involved in ministry as a pastor.

I learned a valuable lesson from my former place of ministry. My lack of involvement in the process of prayer caused me to miss a great number of opportunities. I was not about to make the same mistake twice, and so in my search for a new ministry I became active.

For ten months I worked alongside God. I prayed and kept seeking a place of ministry. I updated my resume, and then sent them out to various churches. For awhile it seemed as if nothing would open up. Yet God was preparing the right place for my wife and me to go. Finally after ten months of searching, a position opened up in a church in Saskatoon, Saskatchewan.

As I reflect on that position, I secured it by being proactive in seeking it out. I hand delivered my resume to the leaders of this city church who were at a camp. We sat down and had some initial talks. Two weeks later they called me to candidate. As I went to candidate I spent time preparing the message and the vision that I believed God wanted me to deliver to that congregation. I made sure I was properly dressed for the interviews. In my part, God did his part. He opened the hearts of those leaders to accept me as their new senior pastor where I served for 10 years. It is interesting that for each month of waiting, God matched it by giving me one year of full-time ministry.

Today I serve at New Life Church in Stonewall, Manitoba, because I was active in the process of

> prayer. It is a great church to be involved in, and has developed my gifts even further.

And so as I end what are the needs in your life, your family and friends, your church and your community? Rather than waiting for a miracle to fall from the sky, God calls you to action-oriented prayer where your needs will be met. Simply because you are involved in the process makes it no less a miracle when the results you desire are found. The miracle is that you have found the blessing of God in your life and as Geoff Treasure writes in his book *Living Right Side Up*

> That is the spirit God wants to see in our prayers. Not a single request and then sulks and silence if a positive answer isn't forthcoming, but a determination to keep on asking, to keep on looking, and to keep on knocking.[33]

Scripture References

Endnotes

PRESENT YOUR DESIRES THROUGH ASKING

Overcoming Barriers in Asking

[1] John 6:37, NIV

[2] Hodgin, Michael. *1001 More Humorous Illustrations for Public Speaking.* Zondervan Publishing House, Grand Rapids, MI, 1998. p. 255.

[3] Matthew 6:11, NIV

[4] *Caedmon's Call.* "Close of Autumn." Cumbee Road Music. 1995.

Setting Guidelines to Asking

[5] Swindoll, Charles. *The Tale of the Tardy Oxcart.* Word Publishing, Nashville, TN, 1998. P. 450-451.

Finding Reasons for Asking

[6] Pierson, Arthur T. *George Muller of Bristol and His Witness to the Prayer-Hearing God.* The Baker and Taylor Company, New York, 1899. p. 167.

FIND YOUR SOLUTIONS THROUGH SEEKING

Seek with Common Sense

[7] *Today in the Word.* Moody Bible Institute, January 1992. P. 14.

[8] Hodgin, Michael. *1001 More Humorous Illustrations for Public Speaking.* Zondervan Publishing House, Grand Rapids, MI, 1998. P. 345.

[9] Luke 8:4-8, NIV

[10] Luke 19:10, GWT

[11] Matthew 11:19, GWT

[12] Matthew 9:13b, NIV

Seek with Determination

[13] Hunter, W. Bingham. *The God Who Hears.* InterVarsity Press, Downers Grove, ILL, 1986. P. 170.

[14] Lucado, Max. *In the Eye of the Storm.* Word Publishing, Vancouver, BC, 1991. P. 216.

[15] Pierson, Arthur T. *George Muller of Bristol and His Witness to the Prayer-Hearing God.* The Baker and Taylor Company, New York, 1899. p. 148-149.

Seek in Partnership

[16] Hodgin, Michael. *1001 More Humorous Illustrations for Public Speaking*. Zondervan Publishing House, Grand Rapids, MI, 1998. P. 256.

[17] 2 Thessalonians 3:10b

[18] Yancey, Philip. Prayer: Does it Make Any Difference? Zondervan, 2006. P. 109, 111.

[19] 1 Timothy 1:15-16, NIV

[20] James 1:26, NKJV

[21] Ecclesiastes 4:9

DETERMINE YOUR DIRECTION THROUGH KNOCKING

[22] Arends, Carolyn. "Seize the Day" from the album *I Can Hear You*.

Knock with Confidence

[23] Ortlund, Anne and Ray. *You Don't Have to Quit.* Thomas Nelson Publishers, Nashville, TN, 1994 (revised). P. 38-39.

[24] Eldredge, John. *You Have What it Takes.* Nelson Books, Nashville, TN, 2004. p. 2-3, 38.

[25] Hodgin, Michael. *1001 More Humorous Illustrations for Public Speaking*. Zondervan Publishing House, Grand Rapids, MI, 1998. p. 101.

[26] Sanders, J. Oswald. *Every Life is a Plan of God.* Discovery House Publishers, Grand Rapids, MI, 1992. p. 29.

Knock with Motivation

[27] Taken from www.wikipedia.org

[28] Eareckson, Joni. *Joni*. Bantam Books, New York, NY, 1976. p. 176.

[29] Graham, Billy. *Unto The Hills*. Word Publishing, Dallas, TX, 1986. p. 119.

[30] Erickson, Millard J. *Christian Theology*. Baker Book House, Grand Rapids, MI, 1983-1985. P. 263-264.

Knock with Discernment

[31] Hybels, Bill. *Too Busy Not To Pray.* InterVarsity Press, Downers Grove, ILL, 1988. P. 74.

[32] Pierson, Arthur T. *George Muller of Bristol and His Witness to the Prayer-Hearing God.* The Baker and Taylor Company, New York, 1899. p. 82, 92.

CONCLUSION

[33] Treasure, Geoff. *Living Right Side Up*. Victor Books, Wheaton, ILL, 1975. P. 127.